Dear God

Dear God

Carmel Reilly

Published in 2007 by Silverdale Books
An imprint of Bookmart Ltd
Registered Number 2372865
Trading as Bookmart Limited
Blaby Road
Wigston
Leicester
LE18 4SE

Illustrations by Leah Barker

A copy of the British Library Cataloguing in Publication Data
is available from the British Library

ISBN-13: 978-1-84509-586-4

Printed and bound in the European Union

3 5 7 9 10 8 6 4

Contents

Introduction   vii

Children's Questions and Requests   1
About Animals   15
About the World   31
About God, Heaven and the Angels   43
Miscellany One   59
Theological Questions   79
Children's Prayers   97
About Home   117
About School   131
About Life and Death   149
About Happiness And Sorrow   161
About Family   179
About Growing Up   197
About Brothers And Sisters   213
About Toys   227
About Worries And Fears   245
About Friends   267
Miscellany Two   281

Afterword   303

Introduction

It has been a fascinating task compiling the letters for this book. I had no idea what kinds of responses we would get to a request for children's letters to God. In fact the letters here cover a huge spectrum, and give an intriguing insight into the world of children today. The children whose letters are collected here are aged between five and eleven, so they cover a period when children are at their most charming and innocent.

A lot of the children here have taken the opportunity to ask God a question. Every parent will know how inquisitive children are. And they will also be familiar with those moments when children ask questions that we find hard to answer.

Sometimes this is because the answer would be too complicated or difficult. When a child asks about where their dead cat lives now, or what will happen after we die, we can struggle to find the right answers simply because we want to teach a child the truth, but the truth is not always easy for a young child to digest.

At other times, we find questions hard to answer because we realise we simply don't know the answers ourselves. We may have long ago stopped wondering why elephants have trunks, why people can't fly or why the sky is blue. One of the joys of listening to children, or reading their questions here, is that they remind us of what it is like to be a child, when the world is a magical and complicated place.

It is only natural that when parents find it hard to answer a question, the child might think to ask the same question of God. Some of the letters in this book seem to fall into that category, while others simply demonstrate the fascinating, innocent mindset of youth.

I have also been interested in the range of approaches that children have taken to the task of writing a letter to God.

Some have taken a formal approach, putting a prayer to God either for something they want or for God to intervene somehow in the world. Whereas others have simply entered into a conversation with God, letting him know what is on their minds at that exact moment.

This means that we catch a glimpse of the world of a child through these letters. Children talk about the things that matter to them – family, friends, school, pets, toys and their community. There are some sad letters here that show the strain of a difficult childhood and there are some very happy and funny letters. Children's lives are as complex as those of adults, and they experience everything very intensely. This shows in the letters they write.

It may help to know how we have approached gathering the material for this book. The book has been made with assistance of a number of schools around the world. I made several decisions early on in the process. The first was to make the process essentially anonymous. The first names given are correct (except in a few cases where I felt it appropriate to change the name for specific reasons), but we do not give an age or place that would enable anyone to identify the writer.

Introduction

We did this for two reasons. One was for simple security and confidentiality reasons. But more importantly, we wanted to encourage the children to be as open and honest as possible. It was explained to the children that their letters might be published, but we also made it clear that these letters were not going to be displayed in such a way that all their friends, family and the school at large would know who had written them. I feel that this has had the effect of eliciting some more personal and heartfelt letters than we would have got if the children had felt that they were going to be 'read out to the class' or shown to everyone they knew.

This does mean that the children's age (and in some cases) sex is not made clear. But I find that the age of the child is often reasonably obvious from the complexity of their writing. A ten-year-old has a much wider vocabulary and more complex syntax than a five-year-old does.

Another issue we had to face was how hard we should try to make this an ecumenical project. There are specific problems in making the idea of 'letters to God' one that bridges cultural divides. The concerns of children are in many respects universal, but different religions have different conventions with regard to the dialogue with a superior being.

The approach I took to this conundrum was to be relatively 'hands-off'. We invited schools from a variety of religious backgrounds to contribute, and in many cases the schools that became involved are multicultural. We also made it clear that any child who didn't wish to write to God should be allowed to abstain.

The end result is that we have a book that is largely drawn from the Christian faith, with some exceptions. To alter this we would have had to be rather heavy-handed in our editing approach and would have had to do a great deal more 'translation'. I think that the approach we have taken is probably the simplest solution to this problem, though it is clearly not the only feasible one.

Finally we had to decide what approach to take to children's spelling and grammatical errors. It is often quite funny to see the mistakes that children make, and some of the 'bloopers' were funny enough to deserve a book of their own.

However we decided that it would be too distracting to leave spelling mistakes in their original form, and have thus corrected in the hope that this allows the 'true voice' of the child to be heard. We have been much lighter in our grammatical editing. We have added a small amount of punctuation, mostly full stops. And we have made a small number of amendments where the original was too confusing or ambiguous. We have also added paragraph breaks to some letters to improve the readability. But we have mostly left the children's words in the exact order that they wrote them.

(As a sidenote, I do suspect that the modern generation of children are worse at formal spelling than earlier generations. I have a particular bugbear about 'txt' abbreviations, but many children seem to regard using both these and emoticons as perfectly acceptable. I have been rather harsh in editing these out. Perhaps they show the true voice of children, but I don't feel it is fair to publish a book that relies too much on computer jargon and teenage slang, so I have focused on using comprehensible language.)

We have sorted the letters into a variety of categories as this gives some interesting juxtapositions. Some of the letters were too bizarre or individual to fit into any of the categories,

Introduction

so we have also included two Miscellany sections to round
up all the letters we wanted to include.

Some of the letters in the Miscellanies are the funniest
here, although some are also rather strange. They can be
dipped into at random, whereas the other chapters read well
as an entirety as they give us a range of viewpoints on
similar topics.

I hope that you will enjoy reading this compilation as
much as I have enjoyed editing it. It has been hard work, but
the end result seems to me to be an intriguing and amusing
snapshot of the way that children think about religion and
the world around them.

Children's Questions and Requests

It has to be said that many young children seem to see God and Santa Claus in the same kind of way, as all-powerful granters of wishes.

A lot of the letters we received were requests of one sort or another. From children requesting new toys and magical powers through to the child who wants so desperately to go to Disneyland, these letters reflect the self-centered nature of childhood. Children expect to be looked after and to be given presents, so it seems only natural to them that they should ask God for whatever they want most of all.

But there are other letters here that reflect children's wider knowledge of their environment. There are children who want to help with new buildings for the school, who ask for money to help out at home in times of trouble, or who simply want God to do something nice for their parents.

In these letters we see the start of responsibility, of understanding that other people's needs matter as well as one's own.

In many of the letters we received, age group was not very significant as to subject matter, but it was very noticeable that the younger children were more likely to ask for something for themselves – for a present or personal dispensation. Whereas the older children had started to think more about the needs of others or to worry about their families.

Reading between the lines one can see that some of these children come from families where there are problems that the child has become aware of. We always pray in times to trouble, and these children are at the early stages of under-standing the difficulties that adults can go through.

3

Dear God,

I'd like to be able to bounce right up to the sky and then come down again safely to land on the ground again.

Yours,

Sally

⋆⊸═◉⁂◉═⊷⋆

Dear God,

I wish I could see a long, long way and see things that were very far away.

Then I could see my granny in her house and she could see me and we could wave to each other.

Best,

Jo

Dear God,

I want a Barbie with a pink dress and wings please. I have seen it on the TV.

It looks like a mermaid.

Judy

⭒━◦✳︎◦━⭒

Dear God,

I WANT TO GO TO DISNEYLAND.

From,

Kitty

⭒━◦✳︎◦━⭒

Dear God,

Can you make me an angel for the day? I'd like to fly around on the clouds and see everything from way up there.

Henry

Dear God,

Our garden is very dry because it doesn't rain enough.

We need more rain please, for my sunflowers.

Isaac

⊶❈⊷

Dear God,

I need new toys. The old ones are all broken, because the baby plays with them.

Iliana

⊶❈⊷

Dear God,

Could you do something really nice for my mum? She works so hard and she gets tired sometimes, so it would be nice to give her a treat.

Thank you,

Rose

Dear God,

Can we have a new car? I don't like the one we have now. It's a boring colour.

My friend Laurie has a car with lots of seats in the back and they can take all their toys because there is lots of space for everything.

I'd like a pink car, with a television.

Thank you,

Ruth

⋄═◉ ✳ ◉═⋄

Dear God,

Can you find lost things? I lost my rabbit called Hoppity on the plane and I'd like him back.

Do you know where he is?

Thank you,

Sarah

Dear God,

We need a new fence because the storm blew the old one down.

Can I have a slide too?

Yours faithfully,

Louise

\-■◉❋◎■-

Dear God,

Please can I have a new bike and a rabbit for Christmas? I like the pink bike that is in the window of the shop. I don't like the brown one because it doesn't have things on the bars. I like all the rabbits but especially the black one.

Happy Christmas,

Samantha xx

Dear God,

Could you make a pink cat? I like cats, but a pink one would be really special.

Love,

Casey

⋆━▶❋◀━⋆

Dear God,

I want my brother's bedroom.

Mine is very small and there is no room for all my toys. But he won't let me play in his room because he says I make a mess.

Can we swap some time?

Love,

Harold

Dear God,

Why does it always rain on my birthday? It never rains on Malandra's birthday and she's only three. I am four.

It rained last year and this year and I like the sun. Can you make it sunny when I am five?

Love,

Jarinda

⋯⋙◉⋇◎⋘⋯

Dear God,

Would you like to come and visit our town some time? We have a nice park and a library with lots of books, and there are some shops that sell toys and other things.

When the Governor came to visit we had a big parade, and a carnival, we could do the same thing if you come.

Tell my mother when you can come and she will send you an invitation.

Best,

Morten

Dear God,

I planted some trees in our garden. My dad helped me choose them and then we planted them together.

One is an apple tree, and there is a fir tree and a poplar tree. They are very nice, but they are growing very slowly. Could you make them speed up a bit.

Or if you can't do that, maybe you could make sure it rains a bit extra on them because they like the rain a lot.

It would be nice if the apple tree grows some apples, but it looks too small.

Love,

Jimmy

✦⟫❈⟪✦

Dear God,

I'd like to have a different name. I want everyone to call me Ariel.

Can you change my name or do I have to tell them?

Love,

Bernadette

Dear God,

Can you get my dad a new job? He hasn't had one for six months and he is getting bored of trying to find one.

I know he wants one and he will work very hard.

Thank you,

Colleen

Dear God

Dear God,

Our school needs a new dinner hall. The one we use is very old. We are saving up money and having a jumble sale, but we need more.

If you can help we'd be very grateful.

Love,

Harriet

About Animals

Children often seem to have a special affinity for animals. They share a relatively simple view of the world, and children seem to recognize animals' instinctive response to the world, and empathise with them.

But aside from simple friendship, children learn many valuable lessons from their interactions with animals. It is often the case that their first under-standing of mortality comes from the death of a much-loved pet.

It is terrible when an animal that you love dies. It makes you feel so helpless and guilty. But as a child, it teaches you about the cycle of life and death, and it makes you start to understand the concept of heaven.

Several of the letters here show children starting to think about heaven because they are hoping to meet up once again with a beloved animal in heaven some day.

Animals also help children to start understanding responsibility and care for others. It is only natural that children are somewhat self-centered, even solipsistic. Caring for an animal is often the first time that they deal with another being in a situation that makes them responsible for that creature's welfare.

Realising that we are responsible for looking after an animal if they are lost or hurt is a first step for a child towards understanding the nature of parental responsibility. We aren't just telling them to cross the road carefully because we like being bossy. We are doing it because we are scared that they might hurt themselves.

For this reason, it can teach a child a great deal if we involve them in the care of an animal. Of course there are other benefits to be had. It is great fun and stimulation to look after animals, whether as pets or in a more rural farming environment. And even those who can't own animals can often take their children to meet animals, whether at the zoo or at friends' houses.

About Animals

Dear God,

Do cats go to heaven?

Yours,

Kevin

→═◦❋◦═←

Dear God,

We went to the Zoo. I saw monkeys and bears but they ran away. I liked the penguins when they went in the water. They ate some fish that a man gave them and he was nice.

I want to be a penguin so can you make me into one? I like to swim but I can only do it with my water wings. Do angels have water wings?

From,

Toby

Dear God,

Why don't animals use toilets? Our cat uses a pink litter tray, but some dogs just use the sidewalk. That's disgusting.

Yours,

Leona

Dear God,

I wish I could go and see my horse every day. I share him with some other families, so I can only go and see him some days.

He is a very nice horse. I feed him and brush him and look after him and I talk to him too.

Thank you,

Leila

Dear God,

Why did you make elephants such a funny shape?

Wendy

About Animals

Dear God,

Our cat got bitten by a fox. She was quite ill and the vet said she might die, but she is OK now. Her leg is very sore and she can't walk very well. She has it in a bandage, and it will get better.

I will say my prayers every night before I go to bed.

John

⟶═◦❊◦═⟵

Dear God,

I wish I had a pony. I could keep him in a shed in the garden. He would be good and I would look after him always.

Everyone could come and visit him when there's no school.

I would ride my pony round the garden, and he could pretend to pull a Cinderella coach for me.

I love you.

Hannah

Dear God

Dear God,

I like beetles, and worms and mud. Some people don't like things like that but I do. I like bats too, like the ones at the zoo, and snakes, best of all.

We sing 'All Creatures Great And Small' at school, and I think about all the animals that other people don't like and things like that.

I'd like to have a pet snake, but I'm not allowed because it might bite people or squeeze them to death. We have a pet rabbit, but I'd rather have a snake.

You must like snakes too otherwise you wouldn't have made them, would you?

Leon

⟶▭◈▭⟵

Dear God,

I wish my cat wouldn't bite and scratch me. I try to be gentle with her, but she bites me anyway.

My dad says it's because she's a tortoiseshell, but why would her colour make any difference?

Best wishes,

Beattie

About Animals

Dear God,

When you made the world, how did you decide what animals to make? You must have had to think very hard to think of such a lot of different animals.

We go to the zoo a lot and I know all the different animals there, and they are all so different. There are animals that swim and fly and insects and mammals and monkeys and everything.

My favourite animals at the zoo are the otters because they are always playing and you can see them swimming under the water through the glass. I try to swim like them when I go swimming too.

Best,

Jerome

❖

Dear God,

Do insects hurt when someone hits them? My dad tells us not to hurt anything, but he hit a wasp with a newspaper.

I'm glad because I'm scared of wasps.

Thank you

Lilian

Dear God,

We have some new kittens. There is a ginger one and a black and white one and two tabbies. They were born under the bed.

Their mother, Maisy, is black and white so I thought they would all look like her. But they all look different. We are going to keep two of them and find a nice home for the other two.

They are very funny. They chase each other about and jump up and down. They climb up your legs and up the plants and they swing off the curtains and the sofas.

Then they suddenly get tired and fall asleep and they are so cute, they all sleep together and nothing will wake them up.

I have to be very careful not to step on them and to be calm and nice with them, and so does everyone else. When we decide which two are staying I am going to help choose a name for one of them, and my brother is going to give the other one a name.

If it's one of the girl ones I want to call her Angelina please.

They are brilliant.

Fleur

About Animals

Dear God,

My dog is very old and she has been ill a lot. We keep going to the vet. I know it costs a lot of money each time, though my dad says we can keep looking after him.

But the vet says she is not happy any more and we should maybe have her put to sleep. I keep saying I don't want her to be put to sleep, we have to keep her alive. My dad says I have to decide because he doesn't want to do it if I don't agree.

I know I am going to have to let her go, because it is not right to keep her alive when she isn't happy any more.

I will tell them tonight, but I want you to look after her when she dies and I want you to know she is a very special dog and I love her a lot.

Ben

⊶═◉※◉═⊷

Dear God,

We have a lot of animals in class. We have African snails and some hamsters and we are going to have a parrot.

I want to bring my pet dog Charley to school, but I'm not allowed because he would bark and he might bite people too.

From,

Taylor

Dear God,

Are animals allowed in Heaven because our goldfish just died? He was called Colin and he lived in a big bowl. I hope he is in Heaven.

Will you look after him? I feed him after school when I have had milk. I can leave his food for you if you want.

I hope you will look after him so he won't be hungry.

Gracie xxx

⋆⫶⊛⫶⋆

Dear God,

I hope there are cats and dogs in heaven. I love cats and I like my uncle's dogs too. We take them for walks on a Sunday.

But my favourites are my cats Rosa and Pedro. They are so beautiful and they like to sit with me and purr. They are such nice animals I'm sure you have them in heaven.

Yours sincerely,

Jeanie

Dear God,

We went to the country for a walk and we got lost.

I was scared of the cows. My dad fell over and they all watched him. It was funny.

When he clapped at them they went away. They are very big but they don't hurt you.

But bulls can hurt you, so you have to run away from them.

From,

Helga

⊷⊶❈⊷⊶

Dear God,

I am scared of the Alsatian who lives down the road.

Every time I walk past he runs up against the fence and barks at me, and it is scary.

Can you tell him not to bark at me all the time?

Thank you,

Colin

About Animals

Dear God,

We went in the car to get our new kittens. I have to be very careful not to hurt them. They are lovely!

There is a brown one and a black one. The brown one is a boy and the black one is a girl, so she is my special kitten.

I called the black one Stella. When she is bigger she is going to sleep on my bed, but now she sleeps in a basket.

I will always look after her, and will never let anyone hurt her.

Jade

⁘

Dear God,

Penguins live at the South Pole, they slide in the snow, I saw them at the zoo, they were eating fish.

Goodbye,

Coimin

Dear God

Dear God,

I have a stick insect.

It doesn't do much but I like watching it.

Why did you make such funny animals?

Love,

Marie

⊷⇒◉✳◎⇐⊶

Dear God,

I am going to have pony lessons. I hope the pony doesn't run away.

If she is nice I will give her a sugar lump and brush her hair.

Best,

Vida

About the World

About the World

In the early stages of childhood, one lives in a very small world. There is one's family, home and friends, and very little else. Small children don't really have a concept of the place where they live, other than that it is their home.

However as children grow a bit older they learn more about the world. They start to realise what a big place it is, and that they live in a particular place, which is quite different to many other places in the world.

This can be a frightening discovery or an exciting one. Certainly it is humbling to realise what a tiny part we are of a world that is a tiny part of the huge universe.

And it is awe-inspiring to reflect on the creation of such a world, the sheer quantity of things and creatures that exist and the number of people living and dead who inhabit this world.

In this chapter we see letters from a variety of children who in one way or another have started thinking about the vastness of the world.

Some are excited by this, and even want to travel the world to see everything that they can. Others seem simply to be fascinated by the fact that there is so much out there, so much that lies beyond their immediate experience.

Learning that our place in the world is a very small one is not necessarily an unpleasant experience. When we are very small, we imagine that everything revolves around us. Just as humans once believed the sun revolved around the earth, we start out believing ourselves to be the most important thing in the universe.

Finding out that this is not true is probably the first step towards learning that we owe others consideration and responsibility.

About the World

Dear God,

The world is very big. I saw a picture of it and it is round like a ball, and all blue and green.

The teacher showed us the tiny little bit that is where we live.

It must have been very hard work for you to make it all and to make all the other planets and space and suns and stars.

You must have been very tired when you finished.

Yours,

Tom

Dear God,

I am going to see my grandmother. She lives in America so we have to go on a plane.

We will be going over the Atlantic Ocean. It is thousands of miles, and nothing but water. Then we will get to America and go to the town where my grandmother lives.

I am excited about going on the plane and seeing things out the window.

Yours,

Michael

Dear God

Dear God,

Is it going to be OK that everything is getting warmer, or is the earth going to get too hot so that we don't have enough water and food and things?

It is scary reading about how all the factories and cars are melting the ice so that the oceans will get higher and come over the land.

I hope you can help us make it better so the bad things don't happen.

Thanks,

Uwe

❖

Dear God,

How does the world stay up in the air?

From,

Georgio

About the World

Dear God,

There are so many things in the world. There are all kinds of animals and plants and millions of people. And there are tiny little insects and mice and butterflies.

And jewels and gold under the ground, and rivers and streams and the sea.

It is amazing to think about. I want to go and travel around as much of the world as I can when I am older and see everything I can see.

Corey

※

Dear God,

If I dig a big tunnel in the garden and keep going straight down, will I get to the centre of the earth? And come out the other side?

Or is hell down there?

I'm not going to do it, I just wondered.

Thank you very much,

Allie

Dear God,

How many kinds of animals are there in the world? There must be lots and lots and lots.

Yours,

Ben

***

Dear God,

Why did you make people all different who live in different places in the world?

We went on holiday and they spoke in Spanish, so we couldn't understand. Luckily some of them could talk English. The nice man at the hotel talked English and he let me ride on the rocking horse.

From,

Thandie

About the World

Dear God,

How big is the world?

Love,

Andi

Dear God,

Could you make a world with a purple sea?

Love

Rachel

Dear God,

You made a very beautiful world for us to live in.

We'd like to thank you for the world.

Best wishes,

Simon

Dear God

Dear God,

Can you make some more dinosaurs? They were cool, but there aren't any left now.

I like stegosauruses and diplodicuses. I don't think you should make any more tyrannosaurus rexes or raptors because they would be pretty dangerous.

Why did you stop making them? Did you get bored?

Jamie

⊷⊱⊙⊰⊰⊰⊰

Dear God,

We had a big flood here last year and our house had water up to the tops of the doors in the downstairs bit. We had driven in our car up to our grandma's so we were OK.

Why does the river flood? Could you make it so it doesn't flood next time, because lots of things in our house got broken in the flood last time.

Thank you,

Julie

Dear God,

How long did it take you to make the world?

The bible says it took seven days but it is so big it must have taken longer than that.

From,

Den

Dear God,

We are going on a journey around the world. We are selling our house and putting things into a storage place, and then we are going to leave soon.

It will be strange saying goodbye to my friends, but we are going to see so many interesting places, and do so many things.

Can you look after us while we are away? My parents will look after me and my brother, but they might need someone to look after them.

Thanks,

Polly

About God,
Heaven and
the Angels

About God, Heaven and the Angels

Children are fascinated by heaven and by the angels in particular. From studying many accounts of human interaction with angels it seems to me that there is a special relationship between angels and children.

Firstly there are the many reports of guardian angels, many of which seem to involve interventions in childhood, when children are so vulnerable to accident or mishap.

Secondly it seems possible that the innocence of a child's mind allows them more readily to perceive angels, and to see things that adults would not recognize.

There are several letters in this section that made me very much want to find out more. Several children casually refer to their angels, as something they take for granted, rather than as something extraordinary or magical. Maybe for these children, seeing an angel is an everyday event, but one that might fade slowly from their life as they become older and less innocent.

It is also always interesting to see children writing about heaven. Most children seem to take very easily to the idea of heaven as a happy place where they will be with their loved ones. But they worry about the specifics of how it will work.

Will their beloved pets be able to come with them? Will they live with their family? Will their grandparents be the age they were when they died or young again? Does everyone live in the same place or are there different towns?

Most children take it for granted that they will be going to heaven. At this tender age they believe that they are good people and they haven't yet become involved in life's many complications which make us increasingly ethically mixed up as adults.

I was also interested to see how rarely children seem to

45

mention the devil or hell. Unlike past generations, we invoke hellfire and damnation relatively sparingly, especially as a tool for terrifying children into behaving themselves.

Personally I think this is a healthy development. We can see from many of the letters included in this book that children are aware of the difference between right and wrong and want to be good (or at least for people to know that they are being good).

But being scared of damnation seems to be a decreasing part of the way that children learn about morality. They seem more inclined to start from the understanding that their actions have an impact on others. And as they meditate on this, the idea of responsibility for one's actions starts naturally to grow.

If the devil has become a mere monster, a golem, on the same level as the witches and ogres of fairy tale, perhaps this is the healthiest way for our Christianity to evolve in the modern world.

Dear God,

How big is heaven? Is there enough room there for everyone?

If it gets too full can you build a new room?

See you soon,

Keith

⋆⇒◉❋◉⇐⋆

Dear God,

I like my angel.

She is silver and very beautiful.

Love,

Kara

⋆⇒◉❋◉⇐⋆

Dear God,

Who is your favourite angel?

Love,

Molly

Dear God,

I painted a picture of an angel.

I'll put it on my bedroom wall so you can look at it.

Thank you,

June

⊷═◈═⊶

Dear God,

Are you the same size as my dad, or bigger?

I think you're probably very tall and nice looking. But a bit scary, because we have to do what you want.

Do you still have a beard like in those old pictures?

Love,

Lila

About God, Heaven and the Angels

Dear God,

What do you and the angels do in heaven? Do you have time to play or are you too busy watching and helping us?

Maybe on Sundays you have a holiday. After church is done.

Lots of love,

David

⋇

Dear God,

What kinds of animals do you have in heaven? I know cats and dogs go there, but it would be scary if snakes and spiders were there too.

Do you ride a horse? What kinds of animals do you like best?

I'm going to have a dog, but not until I'm bigger.

Best,

Simon

Dear God

Dear God,

Are all the angels men or are there girl angels too?

Can I be an angel?

Thank you,

Mara

⊷══◉✳◉══⊷

Dear God,

What is your real name?

Best,

Julio

⊷══◉✳◉══⊷

Dear God,

Are there different bits of heaven? Do people live in different towns and countries there too or is everyone in the same place?

From,

Trevor

About God, Heaven and the Angels

Dear God,

I'd like to see an angel but I never have.

I do believe in them though. My Aunt saw one in hospital after her car crash. She left her body and saw herself with an angel touching her head.

Then she got better and woke up. She says that the angel saved her.

I hope that one day I meet an angel, though I hope I don't have a car crash.

Love,

Charles

•═◦✳◦═•

Dear God,

How does heaven stay up in the sky?

Are there strings holding it up there?

Best,

Yusuf

Dear God,

I saw an angel last week.

I was in town with my mum and there was a mad man shouting. He's always there, everyone stays away from him.

But behind him there was an angel. She looked very sad, but she was trying to calm him down. Eventually he stopped shouting and followed her away.

I know she was an angel because my mum couldn't see her.

Best,

Una

⊷═◉ ✳ ◉═⊷

Dear God,

Do you have telephones in heaven?

And do you have television?

Thank you,

Lonnie

Dear God,

I can hear angels talking in the night. I think they are outside the window.

I try to hear what they are saying but I always fall asleep.

Bye,

Abe

Dear God

Dear God,

When I go on holiday my angel comes with me.

I saw her by the swimming pool, watching me.

Love,

Helen

❖

Dear God,

I had a dream about heaven. It was very beautiful and sunny and everyone was happy there.

Love from,

Angela

❖

Dear God,

When I come to heaven, will I live in a house with my family?

If so can I have a bigger room please?

Thanks,

Joe

Dear God,

When my grandma comes to heaven will she be old like now, or will she be young again?

I saw some pictures of her when she got married and she was very beautiful. It would be nice to meet her like that.

Love,

Dana

⇥✦⇤

Dear God,

If I die young will I have to wait for years and years for my friends to come to heaven and see me?

Love,

Luisa

⇥✦⇤

Dear God,

When I die and go to heaven will I be able to come back and visit people sometimes?

Love,

Frank

Dear God

Dear God,

I know you live in heaven.

Leah

❖

Dear God,

When my grandma was little she saw an angel.

She came into the room and her Great Aunt Jean was standing in the corner with a lady wearing white clothes. Jean told her to look after her mother.

But her Great Aunt Jean had been dead for years. And then her mother got ill and she had to nurse her. She had TB, but she was alright in the end because my grandma stayed home and looked after her.

It must have been an angel with Jean, mustn't it?

From,

Tea

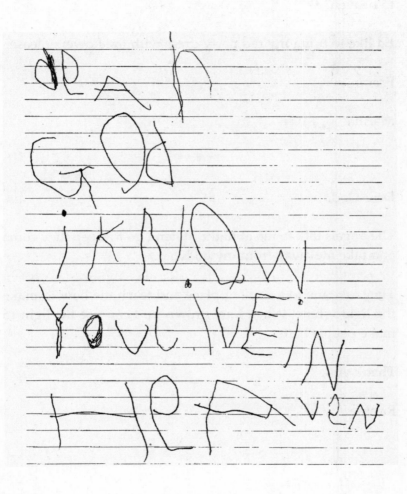

Dear God

Dear God,

Can we bring our favourite toys and clothes when we come to heaven?

I'd like to bring my red party dress with the flowers please.

From,

Martha

⟶▬◉▓◉▬⟵

Dear God,

The angels talk to me at night. When I go to sleep they come and take me away from my body.

They take me to a shining place and teach me how to make the lights shine. When I am grown up I can use the light to make people better.

Thank you,

Ronnie

Miscellany One

Miscellany One

The two chapters of miscellaneous letters in this book collect together all the letters that were unclassifiable into the other chapters.

In some ways these are the funniest and sweetest chapters in this book. A lot of them read more like a train of thought from the child concerned rather than a communication with the Supreme Being.

In some cases this makes me wonder if the writers really understand the task they were undertaking. Perhaps they don't even really know who God is, and simply chatter on to him as they might do to any passing adult, telling him about the snowman they built or the party they went to.

On the other hand young children feel very relaxed with the notion of God and the angels. Perhaps these children have as good an understanding of God as anyone, and know that he does care about every little detail of their lives.

If these children feel relaxed with sharing these little anecdotes or amusing remarks with God, they are on a path to the healthiest kind of praying possible. When we can sit down and honestly share with God everything about our life, not feeling that we need to stick to matters of 'great importance', perhaps that is when we learn to truly pray and to let God into our lives.

If we cannot share the mundane and ridiculous aspects of our lives with God, then perhaps we are simply taking ourselves too seriously.

Faith is a serious thing, but it is also about trying to live our ordinary everyday lives in a way that reflects the glory of God. The youngest child here who shares their *mundane thoughts with God is doing exactly that, and doing it with a touching innocence that gives their letters a real grace and charm.*

Dear God,

I had to stay at home because I had Chicken Pox. It itches all the time. Can you make it stop? I don't like itching and I want to go outside but I'm not allowed till I'm better.

Do you get Chicken Pox in heaven? It's itchy. Today I had jelly.

Lots of love from,

Fran

———◦❋◦———

Dear God,

My uncle put gold coins in his flowerbed and he said that they were pirates' treasure and I had to dig them up.

He had a spade and we dug them up. They were gold coloured but they had chocolate inside. He said it was pirates but I think it was him.

I gave him some but he didn't eat them and I got them all. Can you give him some more?

Love,

Katrina

Dear God

Dear God,
Today we went to the big shop and I got lots of colouring pens and paper. I am drawing a picture of you but I have run out of red.

Are your clothes blue because that is all I have left? I like blue because it's like the sky, which is where you live.

Love from,

Tandy

❖

Dear God,

We went to the fair and I had candy floss but it got stuck on my face. The fair was in the park. My mum got it off but it hurt.

Is there candy floss in heaven that doesn't stick to your face? My mum said it was my own fault and I shouldn't be greedy but I liked the candy floss. I never had it before and I'm sorry it was sticky.

Please say sorry to my mum for making her cross.

Mina xx

Dear God,

Does the tooth fairy work for you?

Love,

Howard

⋯⊷≡◈≡⊶⋯

Dear God,

Do you still like us when we are in the bath? I like the sponge. It makes bubbles when I play with it. I wish there were fish in the bath.

Can you make fish come into my bath? I like them.

Love,

Alex

⋯⊷≡◈≡⊶⋯

Dear God,

Do your legs hurt in heaven? My daddy carries me when we walk a long way, but he says when I'm a big girl I will be too heavy.

Leila

Dear God

Dear God,

Are unicorns real? And are dragons real? Will I meet one someday?

Janet

PS. I like dinosaurs too

◆━◉※◎━◆

Dear God,

I want to come to heaven and visit Blackie my cat who has come to be an angel with you.

Can I come to visit you for a day? I can come on the train by myself.

Lewis

◆━◉※◎━◆

Dear God,

My mummy says not to talk to strangers, but she talks to strangers on the bus sometimes. But they don't give her sweets.

Iliana

PS. How tall are you?

Dear God,

We want to help all the poor children so we are bringing things to school to sell. My mom made a cake too. I helped her.

We are going to wear our party dresses and sing a song about a star. The star wanted to be friends with people but it was too hot and far away.

Some poor people live a long way away, but some poor people don't. We have to share things and we have to share our toys in class.

If someone is using something, we play with something else until they are finished then we play with it.

Sammy

⋆⟶◉⟡◉⟵⋆

Dear God,

Is there an angel in my room at night?

I get scared of monsters under the bed, but my grandma says the angel will look after me.

I will be six soon and then I won't be scared of anything.

Bye!

Alison

Dear God,

When I'm naughty it is an accident. I try to be good and do what I am told, but sometimes I can not. Or I remember something different.

I do not like when I am told to go to my room. So I will try to remember everything I am told.

Please help me remember.

Duncan

＊

Dear God,

Why do princes fall in love with princesses? Do they ever fall in love with normal little girls like me?

Hannah

＊

Dear God,

I wish people could fly like birds.

Hatty

PS. Will I be able to fly when I'm an angel?

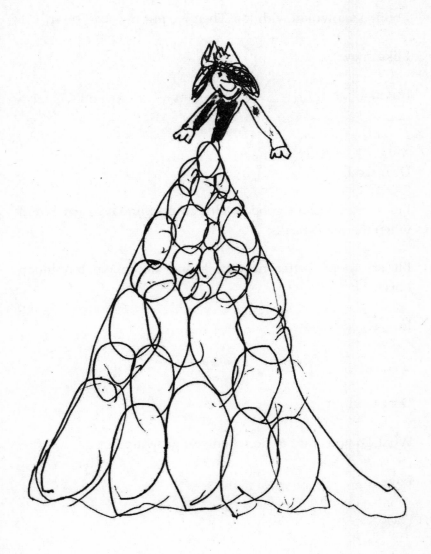

Dear God

Dear God,

I built a snowman with Joe. Then we put my scarf on it.

I like snow.

David

⊷⊱✳⊰⊶

Dear God,

I'm sorry I wasn't good at church on Sunday. I get bored when the man speaks.

I'll try to be better next time and not make too much noise.

Jo

⊷⊱✳⊰⊶

Dear God,

What do you want to do when you grow up?

Love,

Flick

Dear God,

We went to see a film about penguins. The penguins were dancing.

My friend Anna came and we had strawberry sweets.

I fell over and bumped my knee on the way back, but I was brave and I didn't cry.

Love,

Wilhelmina

＊

Dear God,

My favourite colour is blue. I want a blue dress for Christmas.

I am being very good because Santa only gives presents to good girls.

Love,

Sarah

Dear God,

Hello. How are you?

I am fine. I am doing well at school and everyone in my family is fine.

I will pray for all the people in the world who are not as happy or as lucky as me.

Best wishes,

Kurt

⟶▬◉✸◉▬⟵

Dear God,

I want to thank you for everything I have. I have lots of toys and a nice mummy and daddy, and a cat. I like trucks best. I like fire engines too.

Thank you for making everything in the world.

Best,

Thomas

Dear God,

Why does the winter go on so long?

Mel

Dear God,

I asked Santa for a bike but I didn't get one.

Can you send me one?

Luke

My address is 2 Bridge Street. I want a purple bike like Timmy's.

Dear God,

Roses are red
Violets are blue
You made the world
And we all love you

Love and kisses,

Stephanie xxxxxx

Dear God

Dear God,

Number seven is friends with number two, but number three is chasing them.

Monkeys eat bananas, but squirrels eat nuts. They hide them and then they can't find them.

Lee

✦✦✦

Dear God,

I am trying to be good at school. Today I got a gold star for not talking too much in class.

My mother says you are everywhere at once, but how do you watch everyone? It must get confusing for you.

Mark

✦✦✦

Dear God,

I like wearing dresses, but not trousers because it makes me look like a boy.

Love,

Clara

Dear God,

I can answer the telephone by myself now, so if you want to call I can say hello.

From,

Jake

⁕

Dear God,

I don't like tomatoes.

From,

Harry

⁕

Dear God,

I wish I had a tail, so I could wag it when I'm happy.

Paolo

Dear God

Dear God,

We are building a new room in the attic. I'm not allowed up there now because I would fall through. But when it is finished I can go up there and play.

It will have a window and I will be able to see for miles.

Best,

Trisha

⭒

Dear God,

I want to drive a tractor.

Best wishes,

Vince

Dear God,

There are moles in the lawn.

I thought moles would be nice, but you never see them. They just mess up the lawn and make my dad angry.

Could you tell the moles to go and live in someone else's garden?

Thanks,

Troy

⋅⊷▱✳▱⊶⋅

Dear God,

Can you tell my mum to stop playing that song?

Thanks,

Nell

Theological Questions

Perhaps it is slightly hyperbolic to call this section 'Theological Questions'. Children don't know that they are asking theological questions, or alluding to theological debates.

However, most of the letters in this section demonstrate the beginning of intellectual curiosity about theological matters,

Questions raised here include whether or not this is the only universe, the Manichaean nature of the relationship between god and the devil, whether or not unbelievers will be taken up to heaven, the nature of sin, the relationship (or identity) between Jesus and God, and the origins of God.

Put in those terms, these sound like heavyweight enquiries. But when you read the letters you will see that they are simple questions that arise naturally from a child attempting to come to terms with the details of their religious beliefs.

It is inevitable that the inquisitive minds of children will start worrying away at these kinds of questions. For many adults, some of these questions remain of great interest and concern. For others, we long ago decided what we believed and have stopped letting these kinds of details concern us.

However for children, it is important to understand the details of how and why things work. They want to understand how it is possible for God to be both the father of and identical to Jesus (if that is the belief of their denomination) or what God was doing before he made the universe.

Possibly my favourite letter here is the one where the writer asks God if he secretly wanted Eve to eat the apple.

These are the kinds of narrative details that fascinate children. Why, if God was going to be so disappointed in Eve, did he go out of his way to tempt her and to allow the temptation to be sated?

Of course wondering about questions such as these leads us on to more complex ideas such as the nature of human free will, its relationship with our capacity for good and evil, and our responsibility for our actions.

Many bible stories raise as many questions as they answer, but this is part of the nature of religious belief. It is better for us to be questioning our belief, interrogating the reasons for our faith throughout our life, rather than simply receiving pure doctrine, and accepting every detail.

Unless we can question our belief, how can we keep it alive and pass it on to the next generation?

These children are hopefully starting the habit of a lifetime when they question the foundations of their faith, even if the way that they do it in these letters is rudimentary and curious rather than anything more self-consciously intellectual.

Dear God,

Are you watching me now?

Yours,

Glen

⋯≡✳︎⊂⋯

Dear God,

How do you decide who to be nice to? Are you only nice to good people? Some good people aren't happy so why aren't you nicer to them?

Love,

Ruth

⋯≡✳︎⊂⋯

Dear God,

Is heaven nice? My mum says it is like a big garden with flowers. We don't have a garden but Spencer does. His garden has a paddling pool and a big flower. His flower is yellow. I like flowers.

Jamie
xxxxxxxxx

Dear God

Dear God,

Why aren't you friends with the devil? My teacher says he used to be an angel.

Did you have an argument? When we argue at school our teacher makes us say sorry.

Would you let him back if he said sorry? Maybe then he wouldn't do all those bad things.

Thank you,

Lee

⊷⇒✳︎⇐⊷

Dear God

When will it be the end of the world? I know it is going to happen, so I want to know when it is so I can get ready.

I'd like to have enough time to say goodbye to everyone.

Are you going to make another world afterwards or are we just going to all go to heaven forever?

Yours,

Henry

Dear God,

We all drew pictures of what we think you look like and we put them on the wall of the classroom.

I drew you with a happy face.

Love,

David

Dear God

Dear God,

How many angels are there in heaven? Do people become angels when they die, or are angels different to people? Do people go to heaven as souls or as angels?

Does everyone go to heaven, or only good people? Do you mind when people don't believe in you? I don't think my father believes in you, but I know you are real.

I hope he will be able to go to heaven too.

Best,

Tania

⊷═◉✳◉═⊶

Dear God,

Are you really invisible? I'd like to meet you but it would be strange if I can't see you.

Was Jesus really your son, or did you just tell him what to say?

Do you get angry when I'm naughty? I'll try to be good.

That's everything for now.

Barney

Theological Questions

Dear God,

Is this the only planet where there are living things? There are so many planets in the universe; there must be one somewhere with aliens living there. You would know if there is more than this one planet.

Also, does the universe go on forever, or is there an end to it. And if there is an end, how is there? What is on the other side?

Are heaven and hell somewhere real or are they somewhere different?

Luke

⟡

Dear God,

Why did the father like the prodigal son better than his brothers?

Do you like good people better if they do some sins first?

Alan

Dear God,

Who is your mummy and daddy?

Best,

Calvin

❖

Dear God,

How do you decide what is good and what is bad?

Sometimes when I want to do something, they say it is good, but sometimes they say it is bad, but I don't know why.

From,

Cathal

❖

Dear God,

Why can't we see angels any more? You used to be able to see them, but now you can't.

Callie

Dear God,

My teacher has asked me to write a letter to you. I don't know what to say. I have lots of questions, but I know you can't write back.

In the bible you talk to people, but that was a long time ago, I don't think you do that now.

Last week we read about Abraham and Isaac. I didn't understand why you wanted Abraham to kill Isaac, his son. I understand that Abraham wanted to do what he was told, but it was wrong to kill his son. It seems a difficult thing to ask someone just to test them?

Best wishes,

Jane

⋄⟞⟝⟞✳⟞⟝⟞⋄

Dear God,

How many angels are there? Do we all have a guardian angel, or only some people?

I think I have one, because I can feel she is there behind me sometimes.

Love,

Gloria

Dear God

Dear God,

If you wanted people to be good, why did you make some of them bad?

Couldn't you have made everyone good instead?

Yours truly,

Solomon

⤜✳⤛

Dear God,

Who made you?

Carl

⤜✳⤛

Dear God,

Where did I live before I was born?

Best,

Leo

Dear God,

Is heaven in the sky?

How does it stay up?

Julian

—═◉❋◉═—

Dear God,

Did you make any other worlds with people or aliens or is this the only one?

We'd like to know so we can go visit them in our rockets.

Herb

—═◉❋◉═—

Dear God,

What were you doing before you made the world?

Thank you,

Teresa

Dear God,

Do you go to sleep at night?

What do you dream about?

Best,

Jilly

⋄━◎✳◎━⋄

Dear God,

Do you have any other children, apart from Jesus?

Are they people or angels or something else?

Love and respect,

Colly

⋄━◎✳◎━⋄

Dear God,

Which way is it to heaven from here?

Beth

Dear God,

Why didn't you tell Eve not to trust the snake? Then she wouldn't have eaten that stupid old apple.

Did you secretly want her to eat it?

Love,

Tristan

⟡

Dear God,

Why do we have to go to church to pray? I pray at home, and I'm sure you can hear me. Why do we go to church too?

Yours,

Lincoln

⟡

Dear God,

Are you the same person as Jesus or was he your son?

Thank you,

Lane

93

Dear God

Dear God,

Do you talk to Santa Claus about who has been good and bad? You can see everyone so you could help him.

I've been very good this year, so I am going to get some presents.

Goodbye,

Laura

⟳═◈⁂◉═⟲

Dear God,

When I say prayers you don't do what I am asking for. Why not? I sometimes shout but you still don't hear me. Will you answer me tonight?

Mr Robinson asked me to say hello.

From,

Tina

Theological Questions

Dear God,

When we come to heaven, will we be able to watch things that are happening on the earth. It would be interesting to come down and watch people sometimes. I wonder if that's what ghosts are? People from heaven watching the places where they used to live when they were alive?

It will be interesting to find out some day.

Lots of love,

Lionel

⇥▄⬥❉⬥▄⇤

Dear God,

Do you talk to the priest? Does he tell you things I say in confession, or do you just know anyway?

Yours,

Felix

Dear God

Dear God,

Why were you such a lot of different things in the bible? You were a burning bush and a lamb and a lion. And only some people could hear you. Why can't we all hear you or see you?

Marko

Hello God,

Thank you for sending Jesus here to tell us what to do. That was very nice of you.

Jane

Children's
Prayers

Not all of the children who have written to God in this book know how to pray formally. Some of the writers are clearly churchgoers who have been taught to say their prayers at night, while others have a more informal understanding of their faith.

The children in this chapter mostly take a more formal approach, praying to God for what they want.

Of course, some pray for something that they want for themselves. But others pray for others or for resolution to sad events they have learned about from the news.

Children have a great capacity for sympathy. When they understand that someone is suffering they feel a very strong desire to help, and if there is nothing they can personally do, they will often pray to God for his assistance.

One of my favourite letters in this chapter is from a little girl who has come to realise that she is very lucky in her life. As many of us are. Many of us live in peace and prosperity, while elsewhere in the world people live in warzones, or places of terrible poverty and suffering. Sadly the latter group can be within our own societies or countries.

Understanding this is the first step towards a charitable impulse. Knowing that we are luckier than others, we feel the need to help, to sympathise and to offer material assistance.

While some of the letters here are simply personal requests, others give us an interesting view of the aspects of the world that children become aware of. In some cases wars or drought and famine are the focus of their concerns. Others focus on specific stories such as the local disappearance of a small child, or the danger faced by workers at sea.

Dear God,

I pray that there will be peace and that everyone will be happy with their families and friends.

Thank you,

Chloe

——◦✳◦——

Dear God,

When I pray at night I always say thank you for all the nice things we have. We have a house and food and plenty of friends. My family are healthy and we have plenty of things.

I know not everyone is as lucky as me, so thank you for everything that we have.

Yours truly,

Lucille

Dear God,

I pray for blind people. I can see things, but blind people can't and need a dog or a stick. And deaf people can't hear.

Thank you for making me so I can see and hear things well.

Today we saw a rainbow.

Luca

⊷═◉◈◉═⊷

Dear God,

I try to remember to say my prayers every night. I don't always have anything to pray about.

My teacher says that we should just tell you what we have done today. So I will tell you that tonight.

Talk to you soon,

Love,

Rikki

Dear God,

Please make it windy on Saturday, because I haven't been able to fly my new kite yet.

Thanks,

Fiona

Dear God,

I hope the crops grow, and I hope it rains.

I hope that there is no fighting and that we can live in peace.

Your friend,

Dana

⊷═◉⊰⊱◉═⊷

Dear God,

I hope they catch the horrible man who kidnapped those little girls. I saw about it on the telly.

How can people be so cruel?

May

⊷═◉⊰⊱◉═⊷

Dear God,

I wish everyone in the world would be nice to each other. Then there wouldn't be wars and everyone would have enough to eat.

Yours,

Elena

Dear God,

My prayer is for my Aunt Karen. She is in hospital because she had an accident and broke her leg.

I pray that her leg gets better and that she doesn't get too bored in hospital.

We will go see her on Saturday and take some flowers and magazines.

Look after her.

Esme

⟶•≡◉✳◉≡•⟵

Dear God,

I would like to pray for the starving children in Africa. They haven't got enough food and water, so we are sending money to help buy them some. They are so thin and weak.

I hope it rains and they can grow enough food to be OK.

Thank you,

Willhelm

Dear God

Dear God,

Please look after the soldiers who are fighting to protect us and look after my mom and dad, and help us all to get along.

I'd like a Spiderman costume too please.

Thank you,

Lukas

✦═❈═✦

Dear God,

I hope that I never get old and die, and that my brothers and sisters and me will always be happy together.

I hope it is always sunny and nice and that we have lots of nice things.

I hope that we have a big meal with cake and presents every day.

And I hope that the school is closed next week.

Love,

Harley

Dear God,

I am sorry I don't always say my prayers at night. I used to say them every night because my dad said I had to. But now he's gone, my mum doesn't want us to. I hope you don't mind.

Bern

━━◦✳◦━━

Dear God,

I would like to send you a prayer for the men who work out at sea and on oilrigs like my father. They are a long way from home and don't get to come home much.

It is a hard job and it can be dangerous too, so I hope you look after them while they are there.

Lisa

Dear God

Dear God,

Thank you for my guardian angel who looks after me.

Thank you for my parents and my family.

Thank you for the food and water we have to eat and drink.

Thank you for all the things we have, and for the town we live in.

Thank you for everything.

Jordan

⊷►◉❋◐◅

Dear God,

Please don't let the terrorists come and kill people here.

Jake

Dear God,

I'd like to pray for the three-year-old girl who is missing. Her parents must be so worried about her.

If a lady has taken her because she wants her to be her daughter, you should try to tell her that it's not fair. She can't be her mummy because she already has a mummy who is missing her.

Please keep her safe and don't let anything bad happen to her.

Thanks,

Fern

⊷⊶❋⊷⊶

Dear God,

Can you bring us some rain please? Our garden is very brown, and the flowers don't look very happy.

It doesn't need to rain all summer. Just a bit would be good.

Best wishes,

Yvonne

Dear God

Dear God,

My prayers are with the families who have lost loved ones in the war and to the bombs in Iraq.

I don't understand why it all happens, but anyone who loses someone close to them must feel so bad.

I don't know why people have to fight like that.

Yours faithfully,

Truman

━┅◉ ✳ ◉┅━

Dear God,

Please look after us.

Watch over us while we sleep and when we wake up too.

Thank you,

Coral

Dear God,

I'd like to pray for the poor people who don't have enough money. They don't have enough food and clothes and they can't afford to go to the doctor when they get ill.

Why are some people poor and some people rich?

Everyone should be the same, then it would be more fair.

Yours sincerely,

Greg

⊷══◈⋇══⊷

Dear God,

Please can it be my birthday soon?

Thank you,

Jolene

Dear God

Dear God,

I'd like to pray for all the children in the world who don't have mummies and daddies.

They must be sad with no one to look after them.

Love,

Ada

⊷═◉⁕◉═⊶

Dear God,

Please look after the little chicks in the park.

They can be caught by foxes when they are little because they can't fly or run fast, so they need you to watch over them.

Thank you,

Lilith

Dear God,

My prayer is for the people who live in countries where there is a war.

Soldiers kill people for no reason sometimes and a lot of people get hurt or lose their arms and legs.

War is a terrible thing.

Love,

Delia

⊷⊶◉⊷⊶

Dear God,

Can I pray for the Sudan? There are a lot of people who have been sent away from their homes and they are running out of food.

We need to do something to help them.

From,

Glen

Dear God

Dear God,

I'd like to pray for my grandmother.

She has been ill and she can't get out of bed.

Love,

Helen

→═◎ ❈ ◎═←

Dear God,

Please look after all the little children.

A boy got killed when a wall fell on him. It was so sad.

I don't want that to happen to anyone else.

Love,

Sally

Dear God,

I have been praying for the President because he has so many difficult decisions to make and he needs your help.

Love,

Frida

⟶══◉ ✳ ◉══⟵

Dear God,

I am praying for the people of my country. There is a civil war there, and many people are being killed.

We are lucky because my father was able to bring us here. Most of my family escaped but we do not know where my uncle is so please bless him and bring him safely to us.

Thank you,

Poll

Dear God

Dear God,

My prayers are for my family.

They look after me and I love them.

Love,

Stan

About Home

Children grow up in a world with small horizons. Or at least they do if they are lucky enough to grow up in a stable, happy environment.

To most children, their world consists of their home, their family, their friends, their school and, perhaps, their town.

Inevitably their home is a very important place to them, although they largely take it for granted. Perhaps when they move house or compare their home to the homes of their friends they realise that homes are contingent things. We can move to different homes, and different people are able to live in different circumstances.

A few of the letters here are heartbreaking. Some children grow up in such difficult circumstances, in homes that are noisy, unheated, or surrounded by problematic neighbours. One prays that these children will be able to grow up strong and happy.

There are fewer children growing up in poverty than in the past. Of course world poverty is a stubborn problem and not one that has a simple solution, but it is to our shame that any child should grow up in poverty in a modern western country. It should surely be possible to ensure that children should not have to suffer for our political failures.

Other letters here reflect far happier backgrounds. There is a stability and simplicity about the idea of home that conceals a complex organism. The interaction of family, neighbours and friends creates a very specific environment, which helps to shape our early thinking.

It is always interesting to catch a few glimpses into the home lives of others, and that is part of the fascination of this chapter.

About Home

Dear God,

I love our new house. It has two stairs. One to my room and one to the upstairs room.

We will be so happy there.

Thank you,

Troy

⟡

Dear God,

At home we have chicks. The hen laid eggs and they turned into chicks.

They like eating seeds and pecking your fingers.

They are yellow and brown and fluffy. When they are big they will be hens.

Best,

Vernadine

Dear God

Dear God,

I don't like the planes that fly over at night. They are too noisy and my mother shouts at them.

Please make the planes go away. And we need a new house too, somewhere quiet please.

Love you,

Lila

⇥✦⇤

Dear God,

The sunflowers are very big now.

Thanks for helping them to grow.

Vera

⇥✦⇤

Dear God,

Can we move to a new house? I don't like living here, because it is too noisy.

Iain

About Home

Dear God,

Our neighbours aren't very nice. They play loud music and shout all the time.

Can you ask them to be quieter as they don't listen to anyone else when they ask.

Thank you,

Colleen

Dear God,

Can I come and see your house? I bet you have a nice house with lots of things to do.

Bye now.

Harlan

Dear God

Dear God,

The priest says we have to pray kneeling down by our bed at night.

But I like going out to the yard to talk to you. Then no one is listening and I'm not sleepy. It's better to talk to you there.

Is that OK with you?

Damian

❖═◉ ※ ◉═❖

Dear God,

Our house is damp and cold. I don't like it. My mother is sad and won't stop crying.

Ilya

❖═◉ ※ ◉═❖

Dear God,

I don't like the bad boys who throw stones at our windows and kick the door at night. Please make them stop.

Yours,

Matthias

About Home

Dear God,

I hope you are well.

I am doing fine. We always come to church on Sunday. And every night we have to say a prayer. So I talk to you every day.

We are moving house soon, so everything is in boxes. I am worried in case my toys and DVDs get left behind.

When we moved here I never found my bear. He must still be at the old house.

I want to ride in the back of the van but my father says I'm not allowed to. I'm sure the moving men wouldn't mind. I would be very good and help them carry boxes.

The new house is near the swimming pool, so I am going to practise a lot and get real good at swimming.

I'll tell you what the new house is like when we get there.

Lots of love,

Stuart

Dear God,

We moved to a new house and I helped paint my new bedroom! It is pink!

I got paint all over me so I was pink too. I had to have a bath to wash all the paint off.

I got a bit of paint on the carpet so that is a bit pink too now. It's only a little bit though, so it's alright.

Katya

Dear God,

Our street is nice. All the children play out together on the green at the end of the road. Sam has a slide and swings in his garden so we play there.

We live in the middle house, upstairs. It has an old broken car outside, we play on it sometimes.

I'm glad we live here because everyone is nice.

From,

Josie

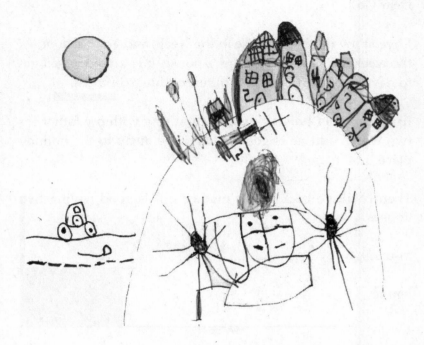

Dear God,

We live in the house next to the church so we are your neighbours!

Love,

Neil

Dear God

Dear God,

I live at my mother's house in the week, and go to school. At the weekend I go to my father's house. It is fun because I get to have two bedrooms, and different things in them.

In the summer holiday I will go and stay with my father for two weeks and he is going to take me away to the holiday place.

Then I will go back to my mother's. It is good having two houses.

Yours,

Jennie

⊶⊷⊷❋⊷⊷

Dear God,

On Sundays, all my cousins and aunts and uncles come to our house and we have a barbecue.

It is great fun because we all get to play together and climb trees and play football.

Our house is the biggest so they all come round to ours.

From,

Ana

About Home

Dear God,

Our house has a red door.

And there is a fishpond in the garden.

Love,

Pog

⬥══❋══⬥

Dear God,

We have a big cross on the wall in our house.

Every time I pass it I think about Jesus dying on the cross.

I pray every night too.

Lots of love,

Tania

Dear God

Dear God,

People have different houses. Some are big or small. Some have gardens. I'd like a balcony because you can drop things off them.

My friend Kate has a house with a pond. There are frogs living in it.

Yours,

Bella

❖

Dear God,

There was a big storm and the tree in our garden fell down. We were very lucky because it didn't fall on the house.

It could have fallen on my bedroom, but it only fell on the fence.

Thank you for that.

Andrea

About School

About School

School is a huge part of children's lives. For ten to fifteen years they spend a large proportion of their time there.

As parents we always wonder what is really happening at school. Is my child happy? What are they really learning? Are they getting bullied?

The mundane truth is that for most children, school is a mix of everything. There are good days and bad days. There are bullies and victims, but over time children usually learn how to cope. Some children have truly bad times at school for all sorts of reasons, but most of them are fine.

If anything, the letters in this section are an insight into children's preoccupations. They worry about who they are friends with, how nice their teachers are, who they will be playing with and so on. They want to do well so that their parents and teachers are happy with them. They worry about letting people down. They look forward to exciting days when something is different at school.

A lot of parents worry about sending their children out to school, so much so that more and more parents consider home schooling as an alternative. One can see the reasoning. But in the end children are all individuals and sooner or later we are going to have to trust them to go out into society and deal with it.

At school they learn how to do this. Sometimes they learn it the nice way, from nice teachers and from good friends. Other times they learn hard lessons, from difficult children around them or from teachers they don't get along with. But either way they are learning lessons that will be invaluable to them in life.

As with many other sections in this book, children in

this chapter treat God as a confidant, but what we discover from reading their letters is a snapshot of the lives that they live.

About School

Dear God,

Our teacher is a very nice teacher. Her name is Miss Price.

She is leaving to have a baby, so please look after her.

Goodbye.

Mehmet

⋆⤙⬡⤚⋆

Dear God,

Do I have to go to school on Monday? I already went this week and it was alright but my teacher says I have to go again. I want to stay at home.

Can you help me stay at home?

Love

Timothy

Dear God

Dear God,

Joanie pushed me over in the playground and I hurt my elbow. Mrs Thompson said it was an accident.

I hate Joanie because she pushed me over. Why did she push me? Can you stop her?

From,

Meera

***

Dear God,

I used to like school, because we had fun.

But I don't like it when they make us sit with cross legs and don't talk and we have to listen. It is boring when they do that stuff.

We should play with the sand and the tables.

Keith

About School

Dear God,

Today I was in a running race at school and I came third. It was raining but my teacher said that it was OK. My mum was cheering but my dad was at work.

He says he will come next time. Can you make him cheer at work so that next time I come second?

Antonella is first but she always is.

Love,

Trudi

──◈◈◈──

Dear God,

I missed the school bus so I walked home. I know the way because I have walked it with mama. I crossed all the roads very carefully and nice people helped me.

When I got home, mama cried and cried and shouted at me, but I was fine. I was very careful, I promise. I know about cars, and I look for them and don't cross the road if I see one.

Hopey

Dear God,

Mr Harley says you are here watching us all the time. You must get very bored sitting through maths lessons over and over.

I bet you are very good at sums by now.

Lois

⊷⊫◉※◖⊰⊷

Dear God,

When I grow up I want to be a fireman. They came to our school and they had a hose and lots of water came out. I got wet but it was ok.

I want to have a hose and get people wet especially Jason R*****'s because he spat in my sandwich.

My mum was cross and shouted at Jason R*****'s mum. She said I have to grow up. Can you make me grow up?

Love,

Gerrard

Dear God,

Can we have lots of fun things to do at school tomorrow? I like it when we go and play outside or take games on to the field.

That would be nice.

Best,

Den

Dear God,

Why does it always rain when I'm walking to school, then it's sunny when we're in class?

It's not fair is it?

Yours,

Benny

⭗✦⭗

Dear God,

I like my school. I have a lovely teacher called Mrs Clark. She teaches us about everything.

We paint pictures and go for walks. Last week she put my picture on the wall in the hall because it was so good.

Soula

Dear God,

How much longer do I have to go to school for? I've been going for a long time now.

I'd rather stay home and watch television. I do read books too, sometimes.

Lots of love,

Gavin

—◦✳◦—

Dear God,

Mr Mills says that I'm a bad girl because I broke my crayon. I was pressing too hard and it broke.

Will I still be able to go to heaven after school if I am a bad girl? I didn't mean to break my crayon.

From,

Sally

Dear God

Dear God,

My name is Beth. I am eight years old.

My sister Terri goes to the big school. I go to the little school. Some days are OK, but some days Tania spoils everything.

Yesterday she pushed my water glass over on my painting and she pinched me.

I put a snail in her bag, but it's a secret. But you know everything so you already knew.

I want to go to a different school.

Yours faithfully,

Beth

⟶══◇❋◇══⟵

Dear God,

I don't want to go to school tomorrow. I want to go to the park.

From,

Orlo

Dear God,

I am so worried about the exams next week. I keep having dreams where I am sitting there and my pen doesn't work, but no one will give me a new pen.

I will take some extra pens. But I'm worried anyway. I don't want to fail and do badly.

Love,

Geena

Dear God

Dear God,

Who makes your lunch? My mum says I can't have a packed lunch unless I make it myself.

Do you have school dinners?

Mimi

❖

Dear God,

I have to do a maths test at school next week.

Please let me do well so my mother is proud of me.

Thank you,

Alan

❖

Dear God,

I hate violin lessons. Do I have to do them?

Eric

Hello God,

I had a bad day. David W***** pushed me in the fishpond at lunch.

Can you tell him to be nice?

Thank you,

Peter

⋆⊷⊷⋇⊶⊷⋆

Dear God,

I don't like Miss Clarke as much as Mr Winter.

After the summer holidays we have to get a new teacher and this year we have Miss Clarke. But she never smiles and she doesn't let us talk.

Yours,

Bernie

Dear God

Dear God,

How long do I have to go to school for?

Liam

⋆⇒◉ ⁂ ◎⇐⋆

Dear God,

I love school. My friends Nina and Jake are always here and we play together.

Jake makes me laugh and laugh he does funny things all the time. And Nina is my best friend.

I like it best when I can do things with Jake and Nina but everyone in the class is nice.

Thanks,

Rita

About School

Dear God,

I want to go to school but my mom and dad don't want to let me go. Kyle who lives down the road goes to school and he says it is great. They play games and the boys play tricks on each other. He knows all the boys from town, but I don't because I don't go to the school.

My mom teaches me at home. I love my mom, but it would be fun to go somewhere else sometimes.

Lincoln

⊶≡⊚ ☀ ⊚≡⊷

Dear God,

I like school, but I don't like walking home because the Johnson sisters follow me and tease me.

I told my mother but she can't come and pick me up because she is still at work. I try walking the long way around through the cemetery, but they follow me that way too.

I shut Tracey Johnson's arm in the gate last week and now they aren't following me, but I'm in trouble because her mum told my mum. But it's their fault if she hurt her arm because they started it.

Jill

Dear God

Dear God,

I have to take a picture of myself to take to school, so I am taking it with my mother.

Miss Hackett is going to put all our pictures on the wall.

Lots of love,

Art

❖

Dear God,

School is fun. We play games and draw pictures and we go out into the school field to look for butterflies.

I play with my friends and we learn about things that live in the sea like whales and dolphins.

When school is over my mum takes me home and I watch CBeebies.

Sometimes in the morning I feel tired and I don't want to go to school but when I get there it is fine.

From,

Isla

About Life
and Death

One of the big moments of childhood is when we first realise that we are going to die.

This realisation can come in a variety of ways. For some children it happens when someone close to them dies, such as a friend, relative, or a family pet. Others learn about death from a more indirect route, such as witnessing the death of a wild animal or hearing about someone else's experience of death.

Knowing that we are going to die focuses our minds on how extraordinary it is that we are alive at all. The miracle of life and of creation is something we should give thanks for every day, especially once our understanding of our own mortality has made us realise how fragile life can be.

The thought of heaven is clearly a great consolation to many children. If a pet or relative dies, they know that they will be able to meet them again in heaven and this lessens the sadness of the loss.

But at the same time, we know that death is forever and that it is something that will one day come to all of us.

This makes the time for which we are alive all the more precious. It also makes us grateful to God for creating us and for giving us the freedom to live in the world and to enjoy everything that the world offers us.

So once the first fear of dying has been overcome, it is knowledge of death that allows us a better understanding of and appreciation for life itself.

Dear God,

Why do people die?

It makes me sad. My great aunt died last week. I didn't see her very much, but she was nice.

From,

Barney

❖

Dear God,

It's amazing that we are alive, because you made us. It's such a strange thing to think about. Being alive is such a weird thing and there are all these animals and plants growing and getting bigger and living everywhere.

Thanks for making us.

Casey

Dear God,

I saw a dead bird in the road yesterday.

I think a car hit it. I'm sorry. I hope it didn't hurt.

If it comes to heaven, be nice to it.

Love,

Gina

＊＝◦＊＝◦＝＊

Dear God,

Hailey told me I'm going to die, because I chose the ace of spades from a pack of cards. She's lying though I know, she's always making things up. But it scared me for a bit.

I don't like the idea of dying.

From,

Rupert

Dear God,

Why are we living here? What do you want us to do?

It's fun being here, but there must be some reason for you putting us here.

Luke

⋆═◉❈◎═⋆

Dear God,

If I was going to be born again I'd really like to be a dolphin. They are brilliant.

Thanks,

Yulia

⋆═◉❈◎═⋆

Dear God,

Do you get old, or do you always stay the same?

Best,

Herbie

Dear God,

I am going to live to be a hundred and twenty years old.

Love,

Otto

⋆⟞⟞✳⟝⟝⋆

Dear God,

We grew some flowers in a pot. They started out as seeds and they got bigger and bigger until they were big and the flowers grew.

But then they went all brown and died. Will they grow again next year?

Love,

Helen

Dear God,

I'm scared that if I stop breathing I might die. How do we keep breathing when we are asleep? It must be some kind of miracle or you make it so we can keep breathing.

I had a hamster that died once. The vet said they don't always live through the winter because they are too small.

Best,

Ruth

✦

Dear God,

My dad has a family tree of all the people in his family. His parents are both dead, but we have pictures of them that he shows me sometimes.

We went to a church in the country to see the graves where his mother's grandparents were buried. They lived on a farm a long time ago.

My mother's grandparents came from India so they would have lived in a very different place. Sometime I'd like to go and see the village where they lived. Maybe when I am older.

Best wishes,

Trent

Dear God

Dear God,

When I die I am going to come to heaven and play with all my friends.

From,

Serena

———❖———

Dear God,

I like living here.

Thank you,

Donald

———❖———

Dear God,

Does everyone have to die or just some people?

Lots of love,

Cleo

Dear God,

How do you decide who is going to die?

It must be difficult for you. When there is a plane crash or something, you must have to be there to decide what to do.

Is it when people are good, they can live?

Maybe it doesn't make any difference because in the end we will be happier in heaven anyway?

Keith

Dear God

Dear God,

My mother was going to have a baby, but something went wrong and the baby wasn't alive.

I feel sad for her because she never got to be alive like me. I hope she is with you now.

From,

Kelly

About Happiness
and Sorrow

Children's emotions are very intense. They rarely feel a mild emotion. They are either up or down, or running all around.

In this section, children talk about things that make them feel happy or sad. The reasons for these emotional reactions vary widely. Some are made happy by simple things like whistling or singing in the choir, or just by the beautiful things they see around them.

Some are sad in a way that might be described as depressed, though one can only hope that this a temporary issue rather a chronic problem.

Others suffer from jealousy, guilt or just general sadness at the state of the world around them.

When dealing with children, we should always remember that their emotions are valid too. It is easy to dismiss their moments of joy or sorrow as childish, but to the child their emotions are very real and can be overwhelming.

Dear God,

I feel sad because I am getting older all the time. I like being little, but now my mum keeps telling me I'm not a baby any more and I have to do things for myself.

I try to be good and do what I am told though.

Lisa

⋆⟞⊜⟐⊜⟝⋆

Dear God,

You must have had lots of fun making the world. There are so many funny things in it.

I like volcanoes and duck-billed platypuses best.

Yours,

Eryl

Dear God,

I got into trouble for giggling at school today. I can't help it. Sometimes someone says something and I just can't help thinking how funny it is and then I keep starting giggling again.

I didn't mean to be cheeky or anything, I just couldn't help laughing.

Best wishes,

Dewey

⊶⊷⊙※⊙⊶⊷

Dear God,

I like nice people, cartoons, books, dolls, the sun and flowers.

I don't like bad people, dirt, guns, things that hurt me.

Thank you very much

Leo

Dear God,

I've been so sad since my grandma died.

I used to go see her on Sundays. Then when she got ill I wasn't allowed to go any more, but we did go to see her in the hospital.

The worst thing is I didn't get to say goodbye to her. Last time I saw her I was in a bad mood and I just played with my game and didn't really talk or say goodbye when we left. But then on Monday my mum said she had died in her sleep.

I wish I'd been nicer to her last time I saw her and said goodbye properly.

Please tell her I wish I'd been nicer, and that I love her very much.

Thank you,

Keeley

Dear God

Dear God,

Here are some happy things:

Birds, dreams, the seaside, drawing things, singing, whistling, ice cream.

Hugs and kisses,

June

⟜══◦✳◦══⟜

Dear God,

Some days I am happy, but some days I feel sad. When I am sad, everything seems bad, and I hate doing things. I don't like playing with my friends when I feel sad.

I don't know why I feel so sad. There are people in Africa starving or fighting in wars. Nothing is very bad for me, but still sometimes I feel sad.

But then I feel happy again, and everything is OK then.

Thank you,

Kevin

Dear God

I think happiness is orange, but sadness is dark brown.

Being angry is red, and fun is pink.

Love,

Polly

⋆⊷⊙⊰⋇⊱⊙⊶⋆

Dear God,

I don't know if I believe in you any more.

I wake up in the middle of the night and I think about dying and about how it might not be heaven. It might just be nothing for ever and ever.

I wish I could be sure if you are there or not. I can't help thinking it's just something people make up to make themselves feel good about dying.

But I do hope you are real. I don't mean to be rude, I just want you to know how I feel.

Lots of love,

Clarence

Dear God

Dear God,

I'm jealous of my little brother.

But I know I shouldn't be. It's difficult because everyone wants to buy him things and play with him, and they all forget about me.

I will try not to be jealous and to look after him, because it isn't his fault.

Thank you,

Ray

⟶※⟵

Dear God,

Today I was sad when I got out of bed.

But now I am happy!

Lida

170

Dear God,

Everyone is happy today, because it is so sunny.

From,

Dee

⋆⟞⊙⟡⊙⟜⋆

Dear God,

Every morning when I get out of bed I feel happy to know that you are there looking after us.

I try to live my life well, and to always do what Jesus would do. I don't always get things right, but it feels good to know that I am doing things for you.

I will try to live a good life for you.

Best,

Georgie

Dear God

Dear God,

I am a lucky girl as my family are so nice, so I am happy all the time.

I can tie my own shoes too.

From,

Luna

⊷⊨◦✳◦⊨⊶

Dear God,

Why is the bible so boring? I like all the stories and songs we are taught at Sunday School, but when the minister reads from the bible in the service. I don't understand it and I get bored.

I wish there were more stories like the one about the lions.

Thank you,

Helen

Dear God,

I sing in the choir. We are learning "The Messiah" for a concert. It makes me so happy to sing it and to feel everyone singing along with me. And I know it is a song about you, so that makes me happy too.

I like singing. I am quite good at it, though I am better at maths and at drawing things. But when you sing in the choir it is fine if you miss a note so long as you try hard to get it right the next time.

It is lovely when we get to sing in the church too because it echoes up into the ceiling. It is so beautiful there.

Love,

Alison

⋆⇒◉✳◉⇐⋆

Dear God,

It is a beautiful day today, and everything looks wonderful. The leaves are going red and brown and the grass is very green. I saw some deer on the way to school, and the sky is a deep blue.

Thanks for all these things.

Tulip

Dear God

Dear God,

My granddad is in a wheelchair, because he can't walk any more. But he is happy all the time.

He tells me that he is happy to be alive because he doesn't know how long he has left.

I'm sad he is old, but he always makes me laugh and smile.

Yours,

Zack

❖

Dear God,

I feel happy today.

Lots of love,

Ian

Dear God,

I think Fridays at school should always be happy day. Everyone should smile, and we should bring toys and games and go outside and play all day.

We should have whatever we want for lunch and not have to do what the teachers say. And the teachers shouldn't have to stay in class if they don't want to. They can all go to the staff room and have a party and we will play by ourselves.

I think we would all be happier if we had a happy day every week.

Yours faithfully,

Alistair

⊷═◉═⁂═◉═⊷

Dear God,

Do you ever feel sad?

Who cheers you up? My family always cheer me up.

If you have a bad day, it's best to think about something funny. Then you giggle and it's not so bad any more.

Love,

Riley

Dear God

Dear God,

I have been ill for weeks but now I'm better. Everything seems wonderful now, because I enjoy all the sounds and noise and everything again, and my head doesn't hurt.

I am back at school and I missed my friends, but now I can play with them again.

It all seems very beautiful. Thank you for everything.

Mario

⋯⊷◉❋⊶⋯

Dear God,

We have such fun at school and at home.

I am always giggling and laughing because things are such fun.

Love,

Jane

Dear God,

I do too much and won't stop, so I have to take a pill which helps me.

I'm happier when I take the pill because I don't get into trouble. But sometimes I like it when I don't take the pills because I have lots of ideas and busy things to do then.

I have to try to think before I do something, and listen when people talk. Then I don't need to take my pills.

Best wishes,

Tristan

⭑

Dear God,

All things bright and beautiful.

I like that, because it sounds so fun.

Brian

About Family

About Family

Families can be complicated.

Some of the letters here are from children dealing with the fallout of their parent's marital breakdown, or bereavement. At least one child is wondering whether he has been adopted or not. Not every child has an easy family life.

But for all of the complexities of families, our family background is the starting point for our relationship with the world in general. We learn about other people, about responsibility and about love, sorrow and anger in the family first of all.

Reading letters about other people's families, one gets a brief snapshot of different lives. One child is worried about his grandmother being angry with him. Another has lost her father in the war. One feels left out when he has to go to bed while his parents stay up to talk. Another is worried because her mother has pushed her forwards in school.

Reading between the lines, one catches glimpses of all kinds of different families. Happy families, fractured families, extended families and families under strain.

But one also repeatedly sees how important the family is to the children who wrote these letters. These experiences are shaping their world. Several children express wonder and gratitude at the luck they have in having a family at all. And even those who are clearly are going through difficult times see the solution as lying within the family.

Families often drive us crazy or make us tear our hair out, but in the end, through our lives, we return over and over to the same problems, the same happiness and frustration, as we try to make sense of the lives we live here.

181

About Family

Dear God,

Thank you for my mother.

She is wonderful. She looks after me all the time and she is always there when I need her.

I am so lucky to have such a nice mother.

Thank you,

Lou-Ann

⟶⟴⟵

Dear God,

My grandfather has been ill, so I can't see him.

Can you make him better because I like going for walks with him?

Love,

Bea

Dear God

Dear God,

I've got a new uncle. Aunt Susan used to be married to Uncle Hank, but now she is married to Uncle Jules.

I like Uncle Jules, but I hope Uncle Hank comes to visit sometimes.

Lots of love,

Gregory

⟶◉✳◉⟵

Dear God,

My grandma got angry at me because I broke her pot. I didn't know we weren't allowed to play with the pot. She didn't tell us not to.

Can you tell her it wasn't my fault?

Thank you very much.

Hatty

Dear God,

My dad lost his job and we are all worried about money. We are doing everything we can to help, but can you find him a new job please.

I will be very grateful and always be good if you can help too.

Thank you.

James

⊷═◈⫛═◷

Dear God,

Please wish my daddy good luck. He is getting married to Lisa. She is very nice and comes to see us sometimes.

I hope we can all be happy together.

Asha

Dear God

Dear God,

My daddy has been so sad since mummy died. I miss her all the time too, but I wish he could be happier.

Is there anything I can do that would make him happy? It makes me sad when he is sad.

I stay with my grandma a lot, so please do something nice for her too. It is good of her to help, isn't it?

Yours truly,

Pol

⋆⊱═◦❋◦═⊰⋆

Dear God,

My mummy is very beautiful. She wears lovely clothes and has red lips and black hair, like Snow White.

When we have a babysitter, she wears special clothes to go out with daddy to the café where children aren't allowed to go.

She wears nice perfume, and I'm not allowed to kiss her goodbye, but I love her a lot.

Love

Glinda

About Family

Dear God,

I have a little brother and a little sister. There was going to be another sister, she was between me and my brother. But she died before she was born so she was never real.

My mama still talks about her sometimes. I think of her too, and I wonder if she is in heaven with you. If someone isn't born do they come to heaven still?

We are all happy and everything is fine, but is funny to think that she might have been here now.

Lucas

Dear God,

I want to tell you about my sister. She is only a baby, so I help to look after her. I read her books and make faces for her to make her laugh.

She has black hair and laughs a lot. When we are old we are going to live together in a house on a mountain and people can come and visit us.

Best wishes,

Lisa

⋆⋙◉✳◉⋘⋆

Dear God,

Thank you for my family.

I love them.

Yours,

Greta

About Family

Dear God,

My mummy and daddy argue a lot, but now he doesn't live at home any more. My mummy is sad sometimes. She tells us to pray so that we will be good. My granny helps us too. She took me to the park yesterday. When my mummy is sad we try to be quiet.

There were orange flowers in the park. There was a big slide in the playground. I was too scared to go down it on my own, so I went down on my granny's lap.

I love my daddy and my mummy and I wish my daddy still lived with us.

Yours sincerely,

Marla

⋯⟨⟩⋯

Dear God,

Are my parents really my parents?

I think I might be adopted. If I am, I don't mind, because I know they try. But I'd like to meet my real parents.

Best,

Stan

Dear God

Dear God,

My daddy always shouts at me. I don't mean to make him angry, but I do. Can you tell him not to always shout at me?

I don't always understand what I have to do. I need a list of all the things I shouldn't do.

I've only got little ears so I don't understand all the things I have to do. Sometimes I do wrong things but it's just an accident.

Trudy

⟶━◉━✢━◉━⟵

Dear God,

On Mondays and Tuesdays I go to Aunt Dana's house after school.

She doesn't have any children, but she looks after me nicely. She comes to stay sometimes when my mother goes out too.

I like my Aunt Dana.

Fred

About Family

Dear God,

When I go to bed my mum and dad stay up and I can hear them. Why do I have to go to bed?

Can you make them come into my bedroom so I know what they are talking about? I like it when they talk.

Boris

◦━◦✸◦━◦

Dear God,

How do you choose what family we are going to live with? I like my parents a lot, they are very good.

My brothers are not too bad, but I like my friends better. It would be good if Joe could be my brother instead.

Love,

Holly

Dear God

Dear God,

I had to go to the big school a year early. My mum is proud of me because I do well at school.

But I miss my friends and I don't like the people in the new school.

Can you tell my mum I want to go back to the old school?

It's not her fault, she only wants the best for me. I know, but I don't like being away from my friends.

Best wishes,

Thalia

⭒⭒⭒

Dear God,

My mother and father met each other and fell in love and then they got married and went on honeymoon, then they had a baby and the baby was me!

When I am big I want to fall in love with a husband and have a baby too.

Thank you,

Colette

Dear God,

When is Mummy coming home? Daddy can't make my breakfast. And he shouts at me before school. Mummy didn't shout at me. When is she coming home?

From,

Bruce

⋇

Dear God,

Last night we went to the park when it was dark and saw fireworks. I had to stand behind my Dad because it was loud.

I got a sparkler but it burned my arm and I cried but it was alright because my Dad got ice cream and we ate some. It was chocolate and I had more than my Dad. He said he was cross but he was pretending.

Joseph

Dear God

Dear God,

Why do we have to have families?

Mine are so noisy.

From,

Jack

⋅➤═✳═◅⋅

Dear God,

My mum is leaving home. She has been away a lot this year. Sometimes I can't remember what she looks like. But she comes and brings us presents when she can.

Now she is moving to another town with a man. My dad says we have to be brave and to stay friends with her. I will be friends with her, but I can't help being angry because I don't understand why she doesn't want to stay with us.

Please help us to look after my dad, because I know he is sad.

Thank you,

Bernard

About Family

Dear God,

My father was in the army and he died. I am very proud of him and I know he is with you now.

Please tell him that we are fine and my mother is looking after us. We all miss him and love him.

Yours,

Celine

———※———

Dear God,

Can you fix it for my mum to be well? She has been ill, and she is very tired all the time. I can't play with her when she is tired.

I want her to be well all the time again.

Love,

Rhiannon

Dear God

Dear God,

My family are the nicest family ever.

I'm glad I have them.

Lots of love,

Jade

About
Growing Up

About Growing Up

"What do you want to be when you grow up?"

Such a complicated question isn't it? And one I still ask myself from time to time! Most of us don't really know what we 'are' even now we are supposedly 'grown up'.

But to children it all seems so simple. You grow up and you become something - turn into a rock star or a footballer, or a train driver, ballerina, doctor or nurse. Like a chrysalis turning into a butterfly, the confusion of childhood will fall away and you will know who you really are.

Of course life isn't like that - although as we go through life we do make decisions and changes that start to define the kind of life we will live. Even if we end up moving through a number of careers, we make decisions such as whether to go to college or not; whether or not to move away from our home towns; what kind of training to do; what kind of lifestyle to adopt. These all have a huge impact on our eventual life stories and self-image.

For some of the writers of letters in this section, the fascinating thing about growing up is the way that they will move through life, becoming the same age as their parents and eventually even their grandparents. These writers look forward to perhaps having children of their own and becoming part of the endless circle of life.

For others, their vision of adulthood is one in which one becomes a certain person. At this early stage this is a rather distant goal, but one can see that even at this age, some of these ambitions may become part of the psychological make-up of that individual child.

And then there are those writers who react to the

199

whole idea of growing up with horror. "Grow up? Why can't I always stay a child?"

Perhaps these are the wisest letters of all.

Dear God,

I don't want to grow up, because grown-ups have to go to work and it sounds really boring.

I want to stay a little kid so I can always play games.

Yours,

Rupert

❖═◎❖☀❖◎═❖

Dear God,

I'd like to be a fireman when I grow up.

They are very brave and save people from fires and they drive a big red truck.

Love,

Louie

Dear God,

My mom was little once. She says she was just like me and that she was naughty sometimes too. I can't imagine her like that. And where was I?

She says I wasn't at her wedding, but I can remember it. I carried some flowers and I wore a dress like a little princess dress. It had sparkles and flowers all over it.

She was as little as me then and we were friends and we used to play together.

One day I will be her mom too.

Thank you,

Sasha

⋆⋄═◉⋇◉═⋄⋆

Dear God,

Old people die. My Nan is very old so she might die soon. It will be a long time until I am old.

I am very careful crossing the road. I look both ways and don't cross if there is a car.

Jolene

About Growing Up

Dear God,

What am I going to be when I grown up?

I want to have a job like my daddy so that I can play games on the computer all day.

Thank you,

Fabio

—◦✳◦—

Dear God,

I don't mind dying. I would like to come to heaven and see you. Everyone is sad when they die, but I don't know why.

I will see you soon.

Lola

Dear God

Dear God,

I want to play for Manchester United. I practise kicking and keeping the ball up every night after school. I can run very fast and when we play on the big pitch I always score.

My friend David is very good too, so maybe we can both play for them.

Thank you.

Luke

⟶◉✳◉⟵

Dear God,

Why does it take so long to get bigger? I want to be a grown up so I can go to the shop on my own. And I want to be able to play with fireworks and use a hammer.

Karla

⟶◉✳◉⟵

Dear God,

When I grow up I want to be a nun.

Love,

Shauna

Dear God,

When I am as old as my mother, she will be as old as my grandmother. I hope I don't argue like they do.

When I have children, I'll let them do whatever they want and not make them go to bed when they are still watching a video.

Love,

Suzanne

⚬⚬⚬

Dear God,

I am worried about my grandmother. She has been ill and she is so slow when she walks. She is very old now, and she gets tired when we play.

I hope that she will be fine.

Lene

Dear God

Dear God,

I want to be a ballerina.

Please.

Rayne

❖

Dear God,

I want to be a doctor because I like looking after people. I look after my dolls, and put bandages on them now. And I help with the cooking too.

I'll be a very good doctor, I'm absolutely sure. Everyone says so.

Yours faithfully,

Vanessa

❖

Dear God,

When I grow up I want to be the man on the TV who jumps out of planes.

Lee

Dear God

Dear God,

I want to be a ballerina.

Please.

Rayne

Dear God,

I want to be a doctor because I like looking after people. I look after my dolls, and put bandages on them now. And I help with the cooking too.

I'll be a very good doctor, I'm absolutely sure. Everyone says so.

Yours faithfully,

Vanessa

Dear God,

When I grow up I want to be the man on the TV who jumps out of planes.

Lee

206

About Growing Up

Dear God,

I keep getting taller. Soon I will be as tall as my dad.

When I am a bit taller I will be able to drive the car, then my dad won't have to drive me to the sports club on Saturday mornings.

We keep track of how tall I am on the laundry cupboard door, and every time we look I am taller again.

Bruno

◦━◦ ❊ ◦━◦

Dear God,

I'd like to have a big toyshop. The biggest toyshop in the world, with every kind of toy in it.

Then me and my friends could play in it all the time.

That would be good.

Yours,

Mark

Dear God

Dear God,

When I am big I want to go and help people in Africa.

Thanks,

Nina

⤙⟾⟬✳⟭⟾⤚

Dear God,

My little sister is a baby. I used to be a baby and I could only lay on my back and roll around.

She has some of the toys I had when I was little. They have been in the attic and I forgot about them. But I don't mind her having them because she is sweet.

When she is bigger we can play outside together but she is too little now. She can't really do anything.

I'm trying to teach her how to crawl. I crawl around on the floor and she watches, but she can't do it yet.

Thank you,

Leila

About Growing Up

Dear God,

I saw some film of my daddy when he was little. My gran showed it to us. It was so funny. He was riding a red bike in the garden and my gran sprayed some water on him and he fell off.

I'd never seen him when he was a child before. I liked it.

Love,

Grahame

✦

Dear God,

Why do we have to grow up?

I like being little.

Lots of love,

Wayne

Dear God

Dear God,

When I am grown up I want to be a teacher. I like my teacher because she is pretty and nice.

I teach the class sometimes when she isn't here. Everyone sits and listens to me. Even Angela.

Best,

Kayleigh

—◈—

Hello God,

I am seven now. Next year I will be eight, and then I can go on the big rides at the fairground.

Yours,

Hel xxx

—◈—

Dear God,

Do you know when everyone will die?

Joe

Dear God,

My Granddad is very old. He has wrinkles. Will I get wrinkles?

Love from

Russ

⊷═◉⊹╬⊹◉═⊶

Dear God,

When I am grown up I want to be a teacher so I can make people do stupid things like write letters to God or stand in the corridor all lesson just because I threw a bit of paper on the floor or go to the headmaster's office every time anyone argues.

Kelly

⊷═◉⊹╬⊹◉═⊶

Dear God,

When I am bigger I want to drive a lorry.

Best,

Fergie

About Brothers
and Sisters

About Brothers and Sisters

We have already had a section on families, but there were so many letters about brothers and sisters that I felt they deserved a section of their own.

The general theme of this section could be summed up as 'Siblings. Can't live with them, can't live without them'. There is obviously a great deal of friction between brothers and sisters, but there is also a lot of love evident - even if for some writers it is more submerged than for others.

It has sometimes been theorised that one's place in the family is an important part of one's psychological make-up. For instance, eldest children are more assertive, but also have more problems with authority, middle children tend to feel ignored, or to seek popularity through humour, youngest children expect to receive all the attention, and take love for granted, and so on.

Of course any simplistic scheme such as this will have countless exceptions. But it did strike me reading these letters that the sibling relationship is inevitably a strong influence on one's character.

The different roles that elder and younger siblings fall into in families are quite similar in many different families. There is no easy way of characterizing this tendency, but the roles that people take within the family are often the roles they take into the outside world.

If one expects to have to fight hard for every inch, or if one only gets one's own way through deviousness, or if one's sister gets more attention because she is prettier, then of course these traits may be carried over into the rest of one's life, not as irrevocable character types, but at least as a starting point for one's psychological growth.

Dear God

So when we interact with our brothers and sisters as children, perhaps we are learning more than it may seem at the time.

About Brothers and Sisters

Dear God,

Why do we have to have brothers and sisters?

Yours,

José

⊷═✳═⊶

Dear God,

I have a new baby sister. She is tiny. Her hands and feet are so sweet. She looks like a doll.

I love her.

Laura

⊷═✳═⊶

Dear God,

My brother says you don't exist. But I know you do.

Ignore him, he is just silly.

Lots of love,

Lucy

Dear God

Dear God,

My big brother is always telling me to do things. He is so bossy. I don't mind doing things my mum and dad tell me to do, but I shouldn't have to do what he says too.

I broke his toy car last week. But it was an accident.

When I am grown up my dad says I will be as big as him, and then I won't have to listen to him any more.

Best,

Leo

~=◦❉◦=~

Dear God,

My sister has been ill. She is in the hospital all the time and she has to have another operation soon.

I pray to you all the time that she will be alright, so you already know that that is what I want to ask you.

I would give up anything to know that she will be well, so please help if you can.

Yours truly,

Harvey

Dear God,

I love my little sister.

She is my best friend.

Thank you,

Cam

⋅⊷═◦✳◦═⊶⋅

Dear God,

Since my little brother was born I have to share a room with
my sister. She is quite nice, but we keep arguing about the
room, because there isn't enough space for all our toys and it
used to be just her room.

I am going to try to stop arguing with her, because my mum
doesn't like it and then she gets angry. We are moving soon
and then we will both have our own room again.

Yours sincerely,

Louisa

Dear God

Dear God,

My brother is always patting me on the head and it really annoys me. So I bit him the other day, but then I got into trouble. But it's not fair, I can't pat him on the head because he's taller than me. So I had to do something to get him back.

I don't usually bite him, but I had enough of him patting my head.

Luke

⋅═◎═⋆

Dear God,

Me and my brother Dave went on a long bike ride and found a cave! It is a secret cave that no one knows about. You know about it because you know everything.

We are going to go back and take some food and live there soon.

Don't tell anyone.

Love,

Roland

Dear God,

I hate my little sister. I'm sorry, I know it's wrong, but everyone loves her, so she is OK.

She gets all the attention and nicer toys than me. And everyone says how pretty she is, but no one says that about me.

I wish people were as nice to me as they are to her.

Lianne

⟶◉✳◉⟵

Dear God,

Can I have a brother?

Not a sister.

Lots of love,

Chris

Dear God,

I have three brothers and three sisters. We are a big family! I am in the middle, so I get bossed about by my big brother and sisters, but I can play with the little ones too. The youngest is Davey. He is just learning to crawl, so he is more fun now, because we can get down on the floor and crawl around with him. Before that he just rolled around.

I'd like some more brothers and sisters please. They are fun to play with, and there is always someone to do something with.

Yours faithfully,

Diana

⊷⊶⊷⊶

Dear God,

My brother is so naughty and he keeps getting me into trouble too.

From,

Gene

Dear God,

I am an only child and so is my best friend Sally. Neither of us have any brothers and sisters. But sometimes we pretend to be sisters.

When we were at the seaside last year we pretended to be twins and everyone believed us. It was so funny.

You're my other best friend,

Josephine

Dear God

Dear God,

Do you have any brothers? It would be neat if God was your brother because you could do anything you want.

And you could get God to make you some new animals when you were bored, like a lion with monkey hands, or an elephant the size of a mouse. And if it was raining you could call God up and get him to make it stop.

Best,

James

⊷⚬▬❀▬⚬⊶

Dear God,

I wish I had brothers and sisters.

I get lonely sometimes.

Best,

Jen

Dear God,

My brother got into trouble last week for breaking that plate. But it was me who did it really. I didn't tell anyone and my dad made him stay in his room all weekend.

I'm so sorry. I know I should have said, but I was scared. Can you make something nice happen for my brother to make up for it because it wasn't fair for him?

I know I don't deserve it, because I lied, but it's not fair for him to be the one who gets into trouble all the time.

Yours,

Anna

-►══◉※◉══◄-

Dear God,

Thanks for sending us my new little brother. I always wanted a brother and instead I got two sisters. I like my sisters but they play girls' games with dolls.

Now Harry is here, I will be able to play football and boy's games with him, so I won't have to play girls' games all the time.

Thanks!

Peter

Dear God,

My sister says she saw a monster in the garden, but she is always making things up to scare me.

I don't believe in monsters.

Love,

Tracey

⋯⋯◉⋇◉⋯⋯

Dear God,

How are babies born?

And why?

My mum went to the hospital and when she came home I had a new sister. She is nice sometimes but she cries a lot. She wakes everyone up in the middle of the night.

But my mother says I did that when I was a baby too, so I hope she will stop doing it when she gets as old as me.

I will try not to get angry about it, because I know she doesn't know any better. She is only a little baby after all.

Lots of love,

Agnetha

About Toys

About Toys

To start with I was surprised how many of the letters we collected were about toys. But on further reflection it is obvious that toys play a big part in the life of a child.

In some ways they are the first friends that a child has. And they use toys to act out all sorts of games and situations while they are learning how to live in the world.

Toys also have a certain kind of status among children these days. They are often competitive about who has which toy - just as adults are about their cars, houses or clothes.

This is perhaps a sad reflection on the consumer society we live in. But it is one other respect in which children's toys play a major role in their psychological lives.

Children sometimes see their toys for the simple playthings they are, and sometimes treat them as though they are alive. So it is no surprise they choose to write to God about those toys, just as they do about their families and schoolfriends, and anything else which plays an important role in their everyday lives.

About Toys

Dear God,

Sometimes my bear is bad. He won't stay still in bed. Please can you make him stay still. I love him and his name is Frederick.

He is soft and helps me sleep but why won't he stay still. Sometimes he pushes me and I fall out of bed but I still love him. Please make him stay still.

Louise xxx

❀

Dear God,

When I get home from school I am going to put on a play with my toys.

All the Barbies are going to be on the stage, and all the animal toys are going to be the audience.

I am going to tell the story and all the Barbies will act it out.

From,

Lucy

Dear God,

We aren't allowed toys at school so I can't tell you about them.

From,

Willa

＊

Dear God,

I've got a puppy in my pocket. He is only little. You can get all of the collection and then they all play together, but I only have a few. I have a black one, one with a crown, and a white one.

Best,

Pat

＊

Dear God,

What toys did Jesus like playing with when he was little?

Love,

Greg

Dear God,

I have a teddy bear that looks like you.

I talk to him in bed at night.

Jenny

Dear God

Dear God,

Do you mind if I bring my camel to church?

My mum won't let me bring a toy to church. But camel will be very quiet and will behave himself.

If he sits in my pocket he can just put his head out and watch. And then he will know all about how to be good.

Thanks,

Julian

⋆⇒◉❋◎⇐⋆

Dear God,

How can I get my toys to talk to each other?

Some of them are friends but they don't all play together nicely because they are naughty.

From,

Ren

About Toys

Dear God,

I have a new Barbie phone, so I can call you up on it!

From,

Liane

⟶⟦◉⟧⟶

Dear God,

The church gave me a plastic rosary, everyone got one. But I have the wooden one that grandpa gave me already.

So I have given the plastic one to my doll Ariel. Now she can say her prayers at night too. She sits on the bed and I kneel down and we can both pray.

From,

Goldie

Dear God,

I broke my brother's toy car. I was playing with it while he was out, and I dropped it, and the wheel fell off.

I put it back in his cupboard, but he will know it was me when he finds it.

I'm very sorry. I didn't mean to break it, it just slipped. It was an accident.

From,

Ant

→══◎※◎══←

Dear God,

You can see everything that happens everywhere can't you?

Do my toys really all come out and play together when I'm not there, like in Toy Story?

I'd like to be able to see them playing somehow.

Love,

Gail

236

About Toys

Dear God,

I have mummy and baby toys. There is a mummy doll and a baby doll, a mummy bear and a baby bear, and a mummy horse and a baby horse. But my giraffe baby doesn't have a mummy. I'd like a giraffe mummy.

Thank you,

Ellie

PS. I love you

━◇✳◇━

Dear God,

My rag doll is getting very old. Her eye has come unstuck and we lost a bit of it when my ma sewed it back on. Her hair is getting worn out.

But I still love her and I take her everywhere.

Yours,

Mary-Jane

Dear God

Dear God,

I have the baby dolls now, but I really need the baby doll theatre to play with them.

Evie has one, so I want one too.

Please,

Kit

⊹⊱◈⊰⊹

Dear God,

When I get home from church I tell all my toys all the things that I heard in church so that they know too.

Then I can go out to play outside.

Love,

Hilda

Dear God,

Can I have a toy elephant please?

From,

Brian xxxxx

PS Please?

⊸━◉❋◉━⊷

Dear God,

Do you like toys? I do.

From,

Ken

⊸━◉❋◉━⊷

Dear God,

I need new batteries for my dancing doll. My dad keeps forgetting to get them, so can you tell him to remember this time.

Thank you,

Isabel

Dear God

Dear God,

We had a nativity scene at Christmas.

I'm allowed to play with the people and the animals if I am very careful. I put them on a farm with the cows and sheep, and the shepherds watch over baby Jesus.

Next Christmas we will put them back in the nativity with some candles.

From,

Geoffrey

✦✦✦

Dear God,

Do you know what toys are thinking too?

Love,

Fritha

About Toys

Dear God,

I found a toy dog in the park. It is made of wood.

Can I keep it? I know it might be some other child's toy. But they have lost it and now I found it, so can it be mine?

Love,

Leon

‑‑◈‑‑

Dear God,

We built a boat in the garden yesterday.

We used the flowerpots and the brush and some grass and my coat. Steve came to kick the pots away but we chased him out and built it again.

Then we went on a journey a long way away.

Then my dad made us put everything back again. It was fun.

Love

Tyra

Dear God

Dear God,

Please look after my toys while I am at school because they get bored without me.

Thanks,

Bob

⟶⇒◈⇐⟵

Dear God,

My doll wants to know if she can be a real little girl.

Can she?

From,

Erin

⟶⇒◈⇐⟵

Dear God,

How are toys made?

I want a dinosaur one.

Love,

Jed

About Toys

Dear God,

Do you know where my remote control has gone?

It isn't in the toy box, and I can't find it anywhere.

The skater won't work without it.

Thanks,

Colin

⋆⋙◉✳◉⋘⋆

Dear God,

My doll comes to church with me and sits on my lap.

Then we go home in the car.

Love,

Laura

About Worries
and Fears

Children worry about all sorts of things. Some of their worries are exactly the same as the ones we have as adults – illness, death, accidents and so on. Others may seem slightly comical, such as the letters here about cauliflower and aliens, although to the children who wrote these letters, their fears will seem just as real as anyone's.

The thing I notice from this selection of letters about children's worries and fears is that children's fears are for the most part quite rational responses to the world they live in.

The two most common sources of fears are from direct experience and from the media. By direct experience I mean that when someone a child knows becomes ill or dies, they learn that fate can be fickle and that this kind of unfortunate thing may one day happen to them or to someone that is close to them. They start to worry that they might become ill or die or that someone in their close family might do so.

This is only natural and it is part of the learning process about the world. It is healthy for children to learn about the sad side of life so long as they don't worry excessively. If the worrying becomes too strong, or if nightmares ensue, it is a parent's difficult job to try to put these fears into perspective.

The other place that children discover fears and worries from is the media. They see the news, they watch films and cartoons, and new ideas come to them this way. Some of these ideas are reasonable or at least realistic. To worry about global warming or terrorism is unfortunately an inevitable part of the world we live in. If we don't at some stage worry about these phenomena, then how will we ever find a way to combat them? It is a

247

depressing fact about the modern world that there are serious problems facing us that children cannot be shielded from forever.

But children can become too worried about such issues on first exposure. Some children will be directly affected by these kinds of major issues, but for others the emotional reaction can go beyond the necessary degree of empathy for the victims. In this case we need once again to try to place these fears into context, to make the child understand that there are positive responses to these problems and that they may not ever be adversely affected. We can also help to dispel any misunderstandings they may have of the exact nature of those problems.

It is rare to find a child who does not instinctively understand that war is abhorrent. Almost every mention of war in these letters is accompanied by a sense of horror and disbelief that people can behave this way. I wonder when we lose this natural abhorrence and start to believe that there is such a thing as justifiable wars?

As well as these kinds of factual, undeniable problems, children can become alarmed by things that they are exposed to in the media (either directly or indirectly through the reports of other children) that are fictional or nonsensical. To become scared of zombies, aliens or monsters seems ridiculous. But a child hasn't yet got the critical faculty to sort fact from fiction reliably.

And even before the kind of mass media we now have existed, children were scared of monsters. Folk tales have from time immemorial depended on our fears of the witch, troll, or golem. Children will always find one monster or another to be scared of. All we can do as adults is to be there to comfort them and to inform them that the monster they fear is not real.

It is not surprising that when children write to God they share these kinds of fears and worries. They see God as an authority figure who can ease their worries and dispel their fears. Reading these letters gives us an insight into the kinds of things that worry young children. God may not be able to write back to reassure these children, so it will probably be down to us to play that role in their life.

Dear God

I'm scared of getting old and dying. And I don't know if I'll go to heaven or hell or if there will just be nothing. Before I was born there must have been nothing.

My grandmother is very old and she finds it hard to walk around. It's a shame because I like her a lot, but everything is difficult for her because she is old.

I wish we didn't have to get old and die.

Yours,

Polly

⋄⊶◉✳◉⊷⋄

Dear God,

Someone told me that we might all die of bird flu. I don't know what I'd do if everyone around me got ill.

Maybe you can make all the birds better, so that they won't give the flu to us?

Luna

Dear God

Dear God,

I worry about my cat Jennie. She goes out at night and she isn't very clever about cars.

Can you ask an angel to look after her please?

Thanks,

Amber

Dear God,

I don't want to get ill again. I hate being in bed all the time.

Love from,

Tilly

Dear God,

Are monsters real?

Love from,

Kelly

Dear Lord,

I am scared about the world warming up and all the ice melting. If the ice melts the seas will all get higher and lots of people in cities by the sea will have problems, and there might not be enough food and things like that.

Is there anything we can to do stop everything getting hotter and hotter?

Yours,

Ute

⭑⭑⭑

Dear God,

What if a comet hit the earth again and everyone got killed. Would we all go to heaven at once?

I saw a film where there was a comet that hit the ocean and everyone got killed by big waves. And my brother told me that that is how all the dinosaurs got killed, by a big comet a long time ago.

Is there any way of stopping a big comet if we find out there is one on the way?

Yours,

Julian

Dear God

Dear God,

Please don't let my mum get ill again. When she was ill it was really bad because she wasn't around and we had to do everything ourselves.

I was so pleased when she came home from the hospital. I hope you will be nice to her and not let her get ill again.

Yours truly,

Fred

◆━◉━❈━◉━◆

Dear God,

I don't like it on the beach any more because Kenny told me about quicksand.

Can we go to the woods instead next week?

Yours,

Toni

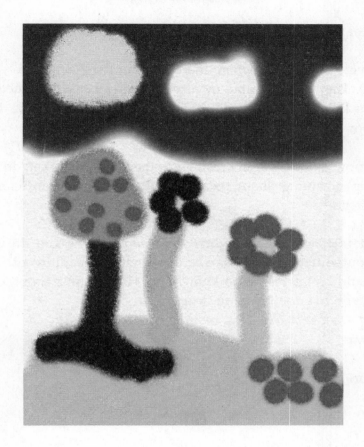

Dear God,

I am scared of the boogeyman.

He waits on the path to Anna's house,

From,

Ella

255

Dear God

Dear God,

I have nightmares where there are monsters coming to get me. They are the same monsters I remember from when I was little and they always hide under the bed or behind the door.

I know monsters aren't real, but is there anything I can do to stop dreaming about them? I'd like to have nice dreams instead.

Do you have dreams when you sleep? Maybe you dream about different worlds where everything is different? It would be interesting to know what God dreams about. Or maybe you don't need to sleep.

Yours,

Mario

⟶⟢◉※◉⟣⟵

Dear God,

I have to be careful of electricity because my dad told me not to play with the plugs.

Can the electricity get out of the plugs in the night?

Lots of love,

Brendan

Dear God,

There are spiders in the shed.

I don't like them.

Lots of love,

Gina

⊶⇒◉✳◉⇐⊷

Dear God,

I'm not allowed to talk to strangers because bad men come and take children away and do bad things to them. I'm only little so if someone tried to take me away I would shout and scream and hope someone hears.

I try to always stay near my parents and friends so no one can come and get me.

I know you look after little children, so I hope you will look after me too.

Best,

Constance

Dear God

Dear God,

Do you send people to hell for not saying their prayers or for lying?

I will try to be good, but it's not always easy.

Best,

Konrad

<hr/>

Dear God,

When I get older, my mummy and daddy will be old and they might die. I would be very sad.

Will we all get to be together again in heaven? If we can maybe it won't be so bad.

Lots of love,

Faith

About Worries and Fears

Dear God,

I hope you really exist. I pray to you and believe in you, but some people say there is no such thing as God. But then nothing would mean anything and there would be nothing after death.

I believe you made us and made the world and I try not to let myself have doubts. I think we have to believe in God too because there are so many terrible things in the world, and the only way we can make the world better is to have faith and to try and live up to your hopes for us.

I know you want people to be good, and if you don't exist then why would anyone even try. I see wars and famines on the news and I wonder why people have to be so terrible to each other.

I believe that we have to try to teach bad people about God and then they will want to be good too.

Love,

Lucy

Dear God

Dear God,

Can you look after my mum and dad so they don't die?

I wouldn't like to be left on my own.

Thanks,

Kate

Dear God,

I am going on holiday but I am scared of planes.

I saw a film about a plane crash and it was horrible.

Please make sure our plane is safe and doesn't crash.

Thanks,

Kyle

Dear God,

This week in school we learned all about nuclear weapons, and about the bomb that was dropped on Hiroshima. It seems so terrible that all those people died. And terrorists could do something like that now, any day. How could people be so evil as to want thousands of people to die?

Did you know people would do things like that when you made us? I think you gave us free will to test us, so sometimes bad things are going to happen, but I am terrified that there might be a big war where terrorists use nuclear weapons and kill people. Because even if you don't die you might get sick from radiation or starve or not be able to find any water because everything will get destroyed.

You can hide in a bunker, but what if your food runs out? I wish nuclear weapons had never been invented, because now they are there someone is bound to be crazy enough to let one off.

I wish everyone in the world would get together to make sure that won't happen, but I don't know if they can.

Harlan

Dear God,

I hate wasps. I'm scared they might sting me.

I don't like the summer because there are too many wasps.

Love,

Bill

⟡

Dear God,

I have a lump in my arm which I thought might be cancer. The doctor says it isn't, it's just a fatty build-up, but maybe he's wrong.

I know about cancer because my uncle died of it. I worry that it can run in the family, so it's something I'll always worry about I guess. I wake up in the middle of the night and lie there thinking about what it would be like to have to keep going to the hospital for all those different treatments.

My mother says I should trust in you and be happy with what I have, but I can't help worrying sometimes.

Best,

Tomas

About Worries and Fears

Dear God,

Couldn't you make the earth so there weren't all these big storms and tsunamis and floods. All those people got killed, but it doesn't seem fair. They didn't do anything wrong, did they?

I know about Sodom and Gomorrah and that they were getting punished, but I don't think that's always why people die in disasters.

I don't think everyone's a sinner who gets killed in an earthquake, it doesn't make sense.

Maybe next time you make a world you could make it a bit safer.

Yours sincerely,

Gordon

＊

Dear God,

Is there going to be an earthquake?

Love,

Sam

263

Dear God,

I can't sleep at night because I am worried the house might burn down again.

But now I'm tired all the time.

Yours,

Queenie

⊷⊷◉⋇◉⊶⊶

Hello God,

My parents say the end of the world is coming and we have to all learn to be safe in an emergency. We have guns and a big barn full of food. My daddy has dug a well so we will have water and we can live a long time here.

But if it's the end of the world, we might get taken up to heaven all at once, before the bad things start to happen.

If the world ends I hope everyone is safe like us.

Yours,

Darren

Dear God,

I don't like the bad people.

From,

Pete

⋅→═◉✳◎═←⋅

Dear God,

Do aliens take people away?

I don't want to get taken away.

Best wishes,

Cassandra

⋅→═◉✳◎═←⋅

Dear God,

Can you make the ghosts go away? They come every night but daddy says they aren't real. They bang on the window.

From,

Lisa

Dear God

Dear God,

I'm scared of cauliflower. I don't want them to make me eat it. It's weird.

I think I like peas. I'll eat the peas if I don't have to look at the cauliflower any more.

Love,

Lulu

⟶◦❋◦⟵

Dear God,

Is it safe in heaven?

Best,

Charlie

About Friends

Children's friendships are strange things. They are forever falling out with one another and then forgetting all about it a moment later. They change their best friends on a regular basis. And sometimes the best of friends can turn into bitter enemies (or vice versa) at the drop of a hat.

All the time that children are experimenting with friends, they are learning about people. They are finding out how social relationships work, and how to relate to others.

They are also finding out about themselves, because your friends act as a kind of mirror through which you can discover how the world perceives you.

The nicest thing is when children feel that they are friends with God, enough so to share the secrets of their friendships with him.

Dear God,

I love Georgia. She plays with me and we went on the swings. It was sunny.

My name is Paula.

xxxxxxxxx

⭄⭝◉❋◉⭜⭅

Dear God,

Today we played it and I was it. Nobody caught me until supper and Anne-Marie fell over. Can you make her better?

She cried but Mum put a bandage on her knee so she was better but I know you can make it go away and not have a bandage on Anne-Marie. She sits next to me in class.

Sometimes we draw pictures and she helps. Please make her better.

Thank you,

From Lisa
xxxxxxx

Dear God

Dear God,

Darren got run over by a car. He is in hospital.

Will he be an angel?

Love,

Tom

⋇

Dear God,

I got very muddy today. Me and Stuart played at making mud pies. Our socks and shoes got very muddy so we took them off.

Aunt Jane shouted at us when she saw how muddy we were, but it was fun anyway.

Love,

Lee

About Friends

Dear God,

I am best friends with Cecile and with Mary and with Lola.

We play together at school. Sometimes they come round to my house.

I like my friends. And I like my family too.

I hope you have some nice friends.

Lisa

⊹⊷◦❋◦⊶⊹

Dear God,

I made a doll for my friend Sally and a doll for my friend Hector and one for me.

I painted them so they looked like us and they can all be friends forever.

Love,

Jill

Dear God,

I'm not friends with Julia and Katie any more. They wouldn't play right and then they wouldn't let me whisper. They started shouting at me so I went home.

Why do these things always happen to me?

Holly

✦

Dear God

I don't know anyone at the new school. I don't like it there.

But I still know all my friends at home. They go to the old school. Next year Jim is going to come to the big school so I will know him.

I will try to make some new friends but I miss my old friends.

Love,

Richard

About Friends

Dear God,

Do you have friends in heaven?

You must get lonely sometimes all on your own.

If you ever need someone to talk to you could come round to our house.

Love,

Wendy

⊷▬◉▦◖▬⊷

Dear God,

I've got a new friend Mike. I met him at the after school club. He is at a different school, but he lives on Station Road, so he is close to my house.

I am going to go round to play on Saturday.

Yours,

Constance

Dear God,

I like my friends.

They play with me.

From,

Patsy

Dear God,

I used to be friends with Lisa. But now she is friends with Mary and Mary is horrible.

So I'm not friends with Lisa now.

Trinny

⋆═◈❖◈═⋆

Dear God,

Can I be friends with you and come round to play?

Louie

⋆═◈❖◈═⋆

Dear God,

I play with Jasmine, but Kayleigh always spoils things by taking our toys and throwing them in the road.

I wish Kayleigh was nicer.

Yours,

Dora

Dear God

Dear God,

I have friends on the computer. We talk about computer games, but I've never met them.

I'd like to meet them some time, but some of them live in different countries very far away.

It's nice talking to people on the computer, because you can find people who know about the same things as you.

From,

Toto

———◦✺◦———

Dear God,

My parents' friends the Thomsons are coming to stay. They are nice, but I always have to play with their son Joey.

He is the same age as me so they want me to be friends with him, but I'm not. He plays stupid games.

I don't like him. I'm sorry.

From,

Tony

Dear God,

Can you send me some new friends.

I'm bored of the old ones.

Thanks,

Julia

⊶═◦�֎◦═⊷

Dear God,

I like coming to school because I can be with my friends. We do everything together. We play, and we do things in class. And we have lunch together too.

After school I play with my brother and sister, but I prefer being at school because all the children in my class are the same age as me, so I'm not the littlest.

From,

Isla

Dear God,

I am friends with Jesus.

We talk together when I don't know what to do. I ask him
what he thinks I should do and he tells me.

Thank you,

Lindsey

Miscellany Two

We have nearly reached the end of our journey. But here is one more selection of the stranger or more unclassifiable letters we collected.

Once again the letters in this section vary from the chatty to the entertaining to the downright strange. One passes through these letters with the impression that one is embarking on a speed tour of the random contents of children's minds.

And what interesting places children's minds are to visit!

Dear God,

My dad has a new car.

It is red and shiny and it smells nice.

Love,

Graeme

⊷⊶◉❉◉⊷⊶

Dear God,

I burnt my fingers on some matches, but don't tell anyone because it's a secret.

They don't hurt too bad.

Kristy

⊷⊶◉❉◉⊷⊶

Dear God,

It is raining again.

From,

Gitta

Dear God

Dear God,

Rabbits eat salad.

Love,

Colette

⟶▬◉▓◉▬⟵

Dear God,

Why do you stay up in the sky? It's nice down here.

Love,

Leroy

⟶▬◉▓◉▬⟵

Dear God,

When you made the animals, why did you make snakes and spiders?

And why did you make cauliflower?

Yours truly,

Marianna

Dear God,

I have a toothache. I wish it would go away.

If the tooth falls out I will give it to the tooth fairy. But I don't want to give it to the dentist.

Brian

Dear God

Dear God,

I am scared of the Queen in Snow White.

But I like Belle in Beauty and the Beat.

Lots of love,

Min

⋆⇌⁂⇋⋆

Dear God,

My baseball team lost again this week. Everyone was sad about it.

Can you make them play better next week. It would be nice to win for a change.

Haruki

Dear God,

I have to tidy my room so I don't have time to write to you today.

I'll write another day.

Best,

Jan

→═○❊○═←

Dear God,

We have to go and live in the big city because my dad has a job there. I'm sorry to be leaving all my friends in school behind.

But I am excited about the new school and all the things we can do there. I can come back and visit sometimes because we will come to see Gramma.

Yours,

George

Dear God,

Thank you for the guardian angel who looks after me. I felt her push me out of the way of that car, so it only knocked me over instead of hitting me harder.

I will try to be careful because I don't know if she will always be there for me.

Blessings,

Tabitha

⊷❁⊶

Dear God,

Do you ever get tired and want to go on holiday?

Sometimes my mom takes me to work in the school holidays when she doesn't have a holiday.

We are going on holiday soon because she has a holiday too. I hope you can too.

Nan

Dear God,

My teacher told me to write you a letter. But there's no point because you know everything there is to know already.

So you know what I'm thinking anyhow.

Yours sincerely,

Calvin (from Boston, but you knew that)

⋙✳⋘

Dear God,

How does electricity work?

Is it magic?

Kevin

⋙✳⋘

Dear God,

Why did you make it so everyone can do different things? Birds fly, fishes swim, but we just walk around. People can talk though, so that's good.

Lee

Dear God

Dear God,

There was a big storm and lightning.

I watched out the window.

Colin

⟡

Dear God,

If everyone lived upside down we'd have to walk on our hands like monkeys.

It would be funny.

Hank

⟡

Dear God,

What is your first name? Mine is Tom.

My birthday is August the 26th. Do you have a birthday?

I take size 4 shoes. Are your feet very big?

Let me know.

Tom

Dear Mr God,

I made banana bread with my mummy.

It was yummy.

Love,

Ines

—❖—

Dear God,

What is the holy ghost?

Does it have holes in it?

Mick

—❖—

Dear God,

I hear the tigers growling in the garden.

Bill says they are not there but I know they are.

Love,

Bridie

Dear God,

Are there trolls living under the bridge in the woods? My friend Anna says there are and they will catch us if we go there.

I want a pink car like the one Anna has got.

Helga

⊹⊱◦✳◦⊰⊹

Dear God,

Thank you for all the beautiful things in the world, all the flowers and rainbows and sunsets and animals, and all the nice toys and food. Thank you for everything you made for us.

Meena

⊹⊱◦✳◦⊰⊹

Dear God,

Why can parrots talk but not other animals?

Thank you very much,

Blair

Dear God,

You should have a channel on the television then you could tell us all what to do.

Love,

Ed

⋯⇒◉✳︎◉⇐⋯

Dear God,

Who is the man who sits with you sometimes?

Sometimes he's there, sometimes he isn't.

Yours,

Tammi

Dear God

Hello God,

How are you? I am fine. I am happy today because it is my birthday next week and I am excited about the presents.

I am going to have a party and all my friends are coming.

Bye!

Lisa

———◦∗∗◦———

Dear God,

I know who Jesus is.

He is the man with a beard.

Love,

Gene

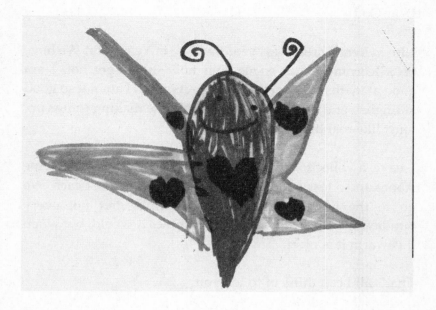

Dear God,

Here are some things I like. Butterflies, flowers, sparkles, wishes, ponies, stars, pom-poms, dressing up things, hairbands.

Bella

PS I like it when the sky is pink too!

Dear God

I am in Year Three. Next year I will be in Year Four. We have been learning about snails, and how things get hot. I am good at maths and can do some algebra, but I am not so good at English and writing stories. I don't like making things up, I just like real things.

I have a collection of things in the shed. There are some stones and a fossil and also the shells I find on the beach. We go to the beach on Sundays sometimes, but not every Sunday. It is a very big beach. Sometimes it is cold, but when it is warm it is nicer.

That's all I can think of to tell you.

Peter

❖

Dear God,

I know it has to rain but it does it have to rain so much?

Lots of love,

Barnaby

Dear God,

If people didn't get dirty, then they wouldn't need to have baths. You should have made people so they don't get dirty.

And children should get bigger faster so they don't have to always do what they're told.

I have lots of good ideas.

Lianke

Dear God,

We are going swimming. I have been having swimming lessons and now I can swim all by myself with armbands.

Soon I will be able to go in the big pool.

Love,

Yuval

Dear God,

Are there people on other planets like us, or did you just make this one? I'd like to go to other planets and meet the people there.

Thank you,

Gordon (Planet Earth)

⋯⊨◯✻◯⊨⋯

Dear God,

My mum takes me to the doctor when I am ill. I had a rash on my tummy. She says it was from eating strawberries.

It wasn't. It was from eating them lying down. If I eat them standing up it won't happen again.

Yours truly,

Hailey

⋯⊨◯✻◯⊨⋯

Dear God,

I love you lots and lots and lots.

Ben

Dear God,

When you were making the world, why did you make animals that kill other animals?

And animals that sting and bite people?

Why are there storms that kill people and lightning and things like that.

Dede

⊷▭◉❋◖▭⊷

Dear God,

Can you make wishes come true?

Glenda

⊷▭◉❋◖▭⊷

Dear God,

My favourite colour is blue.

I like the way the sky looks.

Jolie

Dear God

Hello God,

There is a monster at the bottom of our garden.

His name is Clive and he likes to eat flowers. He hides behind the shed when there are grown-ups there.

Kurt

⇥⇒✳⇐⇤

Dear God,

Do you know what happens to Harry Potter in the last book?

Yours,

Celia

⇥⇒✳⇐⇤

Dear God,

Is everybody in Heaven an angel? I want to have pink wings because I like pink.

Will you send me pink wings so I can wear them when we go to McDonalds. I like fries. They make my hands taste good.

From,

Louie

Afterword

Afterword

As I look back over the letters we have collected in this volume, a few things occur to me.

Firstly, I think that reading children's letters to God tells us about two things. The first is about how children perceive God and their religious beliefs.

But the second and perhaps more notable thing that we can see in these letters is how children perceive themselves and the world they live in.

The things they choose to tell God range from the absolutely serious matters of their lives through to the most trivial details. But even in the most trivial details we can build a picture of how children perceive their world.

Another thing that these letters demonstrate is that children's personalities are very strong from an early age. Some of them are determined, some are emotional, some are sad, and some are irrepressible. But within in a few short lines, many of them have given us a wonderful thumbnail sketch of their own personalities.

I am always an optimistic person. I like to think that the future will be better than the past. Some of the children who have written letters to God for us are clearly living through difficult times. Others are lucky enough to have very happy and stable families and lifestyles.

But with all of these children, there is something in their innocence and directness that gives me hope for them and for their future.

They will still be here after I have gone, and I feel proud to entrust the earth to such an interesting, thoughtful and amusing generation of children.

I hope they make the world a better place for everyone.